THE
SOURCEBOOK
OF GOLF

THE
SOURCEBOOK
OF GOLF

DON KENNINGTON

with an appendix on Collecting Golfiana
by Sarah Baddiel.

THE
LIBRARY ASSOCIATION
1981

Dedicated to Pat who has put up with me and a 36 handicap for many years and who still wins all the trophies.

CONTENTS

© Capital Planning Information Limited 1981. Published
by Library Association Publishing Limited, 7 Ridgmount
Street, London WC1E 7AE and printed in Great Britain for
the Publishers by Bookmag, Inverness.

First published 1981

British Library Cataloguing in Publication Data

Kennington, Don
   The sourcebook of golf.
   1. Golf — Bibliography
   I. Title
   016.796'532   Z7514.G6

   ISBN 0 85365 584 7

All illustrations from the collection of Sarah Baddiel

INTRODUCTION

The game of golf is played in many countries of the world. All the available evidence shows that it is an ancient game dating back many centuries which, in addition to the considerable pleasure and recreation it has provided for millions of players over this time span, has mirrored the social changes of those connected with it. Although there were historical references in documents produced in earlier times it is only since about 1850, some fifty or so years after the game settled into its present structure and format, that literature specifically devoted to it has appeared. In the earlier years, and certainly until the end of the nineteenth century, such literature was sparse. From then onwards, and particularly since about 1950, the flow of new publications has become something of a torrent. The word literature to some, including the distinguished Horace G. Hutchinson writing in 1931, conjures up thoughts of major treatises, of scholarly tomes and of weighty volumes emanating from the golfing *literati* who then, as now, were few in number. But the reality, as in so many aspects of sport and life generally, is that to an increasing extent contributions to this literature are slighter, more ephemeral, and indeed sometimes ill-considered even to the point that many of their authors might well wish, with hindsight, that they had not added to the bibliographic flood. H.S.C. Everard, writing in 1896, one year after the first American golf book had appeared, felt " . . . serious misgivings as to the propriety of inflicting another book on golfers already satiated with the literature on the subject!" Nevertheless, particularly in the present era, much valid and valuable information is contained in works which are undoubtedly less than Literature (with a capital L) but which still contribute significantly to a more comprehensive knowledge of the game in all its multifarious aspects.

The complexities of the literature, and the wide range of other information sources now available, seem to indicate a need for a sourcebook such as is presented in this volume. The well-known golfing bibliographer Joseph Murdoch said in his introduction to Cecil Hopkinson's *Collecting golf books* (1980 reprinted edition) that "strangely I have seen little evidence of interest in golf literature at clubs in Britain, the country of the game's birth and so rich in its history". He goes on to say that "it bothers me to see, at Muirfield and Ganton in Yorkshire, rare and valuable books casually strewn about the club rooms. I would have thought that the Royal and Ancient Golf Club of St Andrews would have an outstanding library but I was disappointed to see so little interest there".

This apparent lack of interest in Britain does appear to be changing slowly, and it is hoped that this sourcebook will contribute towards a better appreciation of the value of documentary and other sources of information in spreading knowledge of the game and its rich traditions. It is also hoped that golf clubs, individual players and others interested in the game, librarians and collectors will all find something of interest within this work. In its preparation, most of the items commented on have been examined and many of the organisations contacted or visited. The sourcebook does not aim to provide a totally comprehensive bibliography of the subject. Rather is it a selective and critical guide which sets out to indicate the most important materials, and particularly those which are most likely to provide answers to specific questions. In the case of books and other printed material sufficient detail has been provided to allow users of the sourcebook to identify any specific item and to enable them to track it down in libraries and elsewhere. In assessing which material to include, the criteria used have involved judgements as to the likely availability of the material and the value of its contribution to a particular area of interest. Where only one or two titles could be identified on a specific topic, as for example on the history of the golf ball, these are included. In other areas where there is a plethora of material, selectivity has been exercised. Only materials in the English language have been included, although it is recognised that there is a growing literature in Japanese and some of the European languages.

Although golf is a pastime to many, to others — a growing number — it is a multi-million pound business. This sourcebook is therefore also addressed to the business sector. Interests in this

2

sector embrace the supply of golf clubs and other equipment and clothing, the tourism aspects, property development and real estate, and the massive growth in leisure and recreation management both in the private and public sectors. Governments, both central and local, and their agencies also have considerable concern with the planning of appropriate facilities. The need for a comprehensive reference guide seems to be proven. Even among those to whom golf is "merely a pastime" there are a very large number who are fascinated by all aspects of the game's history, its personalities and their achievements. Many more spend much of their time off the golf course seeking the "holy grail" of how to play better than they do; how to swing or how to putt or how to "think" their way around a golf course with the unique problems each poses. Many more are interested in discovering new places to play, not just in their own country, but world-wide in these days of cheap air travel. Yet others are interested in the technical aspects of golf course design and planning, in greenkeeping and turf maintenance and in the administration of golf clubs, societies and tournaments.

This sourcebook covers all these and other aspects. The material that has been examined and analysed has been organised in what is believed to be a logical sequence. It starts with the history and development of the game from its early Scottish and Dutch origins, through the biographical literature to the vast number of "how to do it" manuals which have poured from the presses, especially in recent years. These manuals range from the general to the very specific; from overall instruction suitable for the beginner or the low handicap player to texts for women players, for juniors and for the older golfer. There are manuals on the long game and on the short game, and on achieving success with a wedge or a putter. In fact there seem to be few angles totally unexplored in this area of the literature though there does still seem to be an opening for an enterprising author prepared to offer a treatise on "Five wood play for the lady golfer on seaside links"! There is a section dealing with the anthologies of essays, poetry and novels, anecdotes, jokes and cartoons, all of which are a very important part of the game's heritage. The golf business in all its aspects, including planning, land acquisition, course design and maintenance, the administration of the game, golf club management and guides to golf courses, also has a chapter devoted to it. A further chapter brings together reference works including encyclopaedias, dictionaries, statistical information, the rules of golf, bibliographic material and the golfing magazines. Finally the work of the golf organisations, particularly those in Britain and the United States, is described. They contribute much to the game, not least in the provision of information on many of its facets.

It is recognised that the judgements which have had to be exercised in placing material within a particular chapter will not always suit every individual wishing to use this guide. To overcome the problems this may produce, detailed indexes have been provided. These facilitate access to titles of books and other works mentioned and to the subjects covered and the individuals named, whether they are authors, editors or simply subjects. Each chapter consists of a narrative section, highlighting what are believed to be the more important sources, and a comprehensive annotated bibliography of relevant items. The detail in these bibliographies includes, as far as possible, author, title and sub-title, place of publication, name of publisher and date of publication. Details of editions are usually given where known, and the number of pages is normally included to give the user some indication of the depth of treatment provided. Many entries also include information on series, where appropriate, and have a brief note on the contents of the document.

Except in Chapter 2, all entries in the bibliographies are listed in alphabetical order of authors' names. In Chapter 2 the references are organised broadly into two sections with collected biography followed by individual biographies, the latter arranged under the name of the biographee. In Chapter 7 the names, addresses and telephone numbers of relevant organisations are listed after the narrative section, with a brief bibliography of items (not listed elsewhere) which are published by one or other of the organisations. Where there are up to three joint authors to an individual work these are given in the heading of the entry, but where there are four or more the style of *and others* is preferred. In all cases joint authorships are listed after all other items by the single author.

It is a particularly noticeable feature of the golfing literature that many of the books published have alternative titles when issued in different markets — usually the British and North American markets. As far as possible these variations have been noted in the entries, and in general the first title given is the one which was used in the original market. In other words, if the book appeared in Britain before publication in the United States, the British title is preferred, and *vice versa*. If simultaneous publica-

4

tion seems to have taken place under different titles then the British title has been chosen.

In the process of compiling the material included in this sourcebook many organisations and individuals have been contacted and consulted. In addition, the resources of many libraries have been used. These include the London Library, Greenwich Libraries, the Edinburgh City Libraries, the Kent County Library (Tunbridge Wells Division), the Sports Council Information Centre, the Greater London Council Research Library and the Sports Documentation Centre of the University of Birmingham. The help of librarians at these institutions is gratefully acknowledged, as is the help received from many who supplied information on their organisation and its functions and services. Assistance has also been received from Barney Underwood, of the Hawkhurst Golf Club, Ted Watkinson, of True Temper Inc, Archie Baird, of the Gullane Golf Museum, Hope Letters of North Berwick and Messrs Scott and Breen of the Royal and Ancient Golf Club of St Andrews. Their help has been much appreciated. The curator/librarian of the United States Golf Association, Ms. Janet Seagle, also provided much important and interesting material for which the author is very grateful; but most helpful of all was the superb bibliographical work of Joseph Murdoch, which has provided an invaluable check list to the many queries which arise in a project such as this. Any errors, omissions or misjudgements are solely the responsibility of the author, who will be pleased to be advised of these so that possible future editions can be improved.

Tunbridge Wells, England
January 1981

5

CHAPTER ONE

THE
HISTORY OF GOLF

It is generally accepted that the game of golf originated between five and six hundred years ago. Although many believe that its earliest beginnings were in Holland, most golfers regard Scotland as the real home of the game, and there is little doubt that this is true of the game as it is played today. Many of the earliest references to the game are pictorial — a stained-glass roundel in Gloucester Cathedral in England is claimed as the first — and there are many other documented references in Scottish government papers, in the more popular literature, in poetry and elsewhere. This volume is not the place to examine or pass judgement on these early claims. Nor is it appropriate to give more than passing attention to these early fugitive items, which are listed comprehensively elsewhere. This sourcebook will concentrate on identifying these key historical works, by important and well-qualified writers, so that those interested in pursuing the "prehistoric period" of golfing history may do so.

In general, the year 1850 has been taken as a starting point since it is usually agreed that the development of the golfing *literature* began at around this time. It is a literature which has become as rich and prolific as that of any game played, though cricketers may dispute this statement. Murdoch and Seagle in their introduction to *Golf: a guide to information sources* (1979) say that "it is indeed amazing that so much has been written about a rather simple game . . . one hits a small ball from a designated starting point with one of several clubs to a target which is a small hole in the ground of varying distances from the start . . . one attempts to accomplish this in as few strokes as possible". "Very simple . . ." they also say, but the vast majority of those who play golf, or attempt to do, will testify that it is a game with endless variations and complications, played on every type of terrain, which means that no single shot is exactly similar to any other. Golf is today played world wide — in deserts and on ice-caps — as well as in the more beautiful surroundings of some of the world's famous courses. Even in the more hospitable climates it is played in all types of weather, in high winds and light breezes, in wet weather and dry, and its unique system of handicapping and provision of standard scratch scores for golf courses means that it has a unique feature in that it is possible for people of very different capabilities to play together and enjoy a competitive contest.

These special qualities have challenged many in the playing sense. Luckily some of those who have taken to the game have also been accomplished scholars and authors, and many fine books and other writings have appeared on the subject. This is not to say that all (or even the majority) of the golfing literature is of a high standard in the literary sense but it has undoubtedly been more fortunate than most other sports and many other subject fields of perhaps more weighty significance.

This first chapter on the history and development of the game includes a reasonable proportion of the older material written in the nineteenth and early twentieth centuries, even when strictly it might well be classified elsewhere in this sourcebook. An example of this licence is the inclusion here of H.B. Farnie's *The golfer's manual* (1857) which is widely recognised as the earliest separate textbook on the game to be published. It appeared originally under the author's pseudonym of "A keen hand" and was subtitled "an historical and descriptive account of the national game of Scotland". It covers every aspect of the game from its early history to a discussion of its philosophy, and includes plenty of instructional hints. Second and third editions appeared in 1862 and 1870, and it was reprinted in a handsome special edition by the Dropmore Press of London in 1947.

Another landmark of the early literature was Robert Clark's *Golf: a royal and ancient game,* which appeared in 1875. Clark was an Edinburgh printer who put together an immensely interesting volume including much historical material and some biographical sketches. The book also included many extracts from the minutes of the earliest golf clubs. It is regarded still as a key source book to early golf history and practice. The second edition appeared in 1893, and facsimile reprints of this have been issued in Britain in 1975 and in the United States in the following year. Robert Forgan's *Golfer's handbook* (1881) included information

on the history of the game, hints to beginners, feats of champion golfers, and lists of the leading clubs and their office bearers. Forgan was the founder of a famous club-making firm at St Andrews and his brief, but important, book ran to a number of editions. J.L. Stewart's *Golfiana miscellanea* (1887) brought together within the same covers a number of early pamphlets and other very early works, but lacked original material.

On the other hand, Sir Walter Simpson's *The art of golf* (1887) was an amusing, entertaining and highly original work which was innovative in its use of instructional photographs. Simpson was a former captain of the Honourable Company of Edinburgh Golfers, and his prose is full of delicious quotes. Two typical samples will indicate what the reader will find in the pages of this book. On page 19, Simpson says ". . . links are too barren for cultivation, but sheep, rabbits, geese and professionals pick up a precarious living on them . . . " In another passage he says "I have seen a golfer very angry at getting into a bunker by killing a bird and rewards of as much as ten shillings have been offered for boys maimed on the links". Simpson also opined that "although

9

unsuited to the novelist golf lends itself readily to the dreaming of scenes in which the dreamer is the hero". Apart from the golf instruction and homespun philosophy contained within its pages *The art of golf* throws a good deal of light on the rigid class system and social differences of the period.

The first book written by the emerging professional golfers was *The game of golf* (1896) by Willie Park, Jr. This book included historical material and instruction and also technical information on course construction and upkeep, reflecting the fact that many early professionals were also responsible for greenkeeping and course maintenance.

Horace G. Hutchinson, who was himself a fine amateur golfer, produced the first of his many splendid books on all aspects of the game in 1890. *Golf*, in the Badminton Library of Sports and Pastimes, has come to be regarded as one of the finest golf books ever produced. It is a delightful book with interesting pictures and many amusing anecdotes. As was typical of the time, it included historical and biographical material as well as hints on technique. Hutchinson's books were published on both sides of the Atlantic, and he was the most prolific golfing writer until the advent of Bernard Darwin. Other important titles by Hutchinson were *The book of golf and golfers* (1899) and *Fifty years of golf* (1919). The former was a comprehensive treatise on more aspects of the game and had a distinguished list of contributors including H.H. Hilton, J.H. Taylor and Messrs. Sutton and Sons, the grass seed firm, on the arts of greenkeeping. Horace Hutchinson was the first Englishman to become captain of the Royal and Ancient, and one of his final published essays was a chapter on "The literature of the game" which appeared in Joyce Wethered's *The game of golf* in 1931. There was no-one better qualified to write on this topic at that time.

Before coming to more recent histories, mention should be made of J.H. Taylor's *Taylor on golf* (1902) which was a compendium on most aspects of the game including practical hints on playing golf. *The royal and ancient game of golf* (1912) by Harold H. Hilton and Garden G. Smith is also an excellent work, handsomely produced and valuable on the second-hand market today. The book was published by the magazine *Golf Illustrated* and was comprehensive in its treatment of the game. It also included a listing of golf books published to that date. Two other works from this period are worthy of mention. One is *Originaes golfianae*, edited by Arthur Taylor and subtitled "The birth of golf and its

10

early childhood as revealed in a chance-discovered manuscript from a Scottish monastery". The other is the work of an eminent American golf course architect, Charles B. MacDonald, who produced an excellent volume entitled *Scotland's gift – golf* in 1928.

Joyce Wethered's *The game of golf* (1931) has already been mentioned, and in addition to the contribution by Hutchinson this excellent book included sections by her brother Roger Wethered and by Bernard Darwin. Darwin's own major contributions to the historical literature on golf were *Golf between the wars* (1944), regarded by many critics as one of his best works, and the brief *British golf* (1946), published just after the end of World War II. But perhaps the most important of all was *A history of golf in Britain* (1952) to which Darwin was a senior contributor. This work has been called "one of the great modern day classics of golf literature", and is often cited by later authors. It covers the game, its implements, and players over the centuries. Other contributors to this important book included Sir Guy Campbell, Henry Longhurst, Henry Cotton and Leonard Crawley. Three years after this volume was published, another major work appeared from the pen of Robert Browning. Browning's *A history of golf* (1955), apart from being well-written, was particularly good on the origins of the game.

Eight years later Charles Price's *The world of golf* (1963) was published. It too was an excellent book; one of the best of its type. Another American author, Nevin H. Gibson, produced a collection of superb golfing photographs under the title of *A pictorial history of golf* in 1968, and a second edition of this work appeared in 1974 in the United States. Former Open Champion Henry Cotton produced a similar volume, *Golf: a pictorial history* (1975). Other British authors making useful contributions to the historical literature include Tom Scott with his *Story of golf from its origins to the present day* (1972), which is particularly good on the beginnings of the game, and Geoffrey Cousins, whose *Golf in Britain* (1975) looks at the social aspects of the game and its development. This latter book includes a brief, but useful, annotated bibliography.

The progress of the ladies' golf game is usually covered in the general histories of the game, but there are also a few works dealing specifically with it. May Hezlet's *Ladies golf* (1904) was probably the first book on women's golf, and contained instructional as well as more general material. A second edition of the book appeared in 1907. Enid Wilson's *A gallery of women golfers* (1961) was also written by a noted lady golfer of her time. Lewine Mair's *The Dunlop lady golfers' companion* (1980) covers the entire history of the women's game as well as discussing topics of current concern.

Professional golf has also generated its own historical literature. Geoffrey Cousins' *Lords of the links* (1977) is the story of the professional game, while Mark McCormack traces the development of the United States professional golf tour from 1946 in his *Wonderful world of professional golf* (1973). Many − in fact the large majority of professional golfers − are unconcerned with the major tournaments, and operate as teachers of the game and as retailers of golfing equipment at club level. Their associations, whose activities are described in more detail in Chapter 7, have exerted and continue to exert considerable influence on the game. The Professional Golfers Association of America has been fortunate in having the knowledgeable Herb Graffis to prepare its history. His book *The PGA* (1975) is a detailed and authoritative history of the Association. The American professional circuit of tournaments known as "the tour" is described in Al Barkow's *Golf's golden grind* (1974), and Christopher Keane covers one particular year in some detail in his book *The tour,* also published in 1974. Nevin Gibson's *Great moments in golf* (1973) records important events in the game's history, particularly recent ones involving present-day players.

The key events of the United States golfing calendar are the Masters Tournament held in Augusta, Georgia each April, the United States PGA Championship, and the United States Open. All these events have generated a considerable literature of their own. The Masters has developed something of an aura by means of shrewd promotion and expert public relations as well as by the quality of the golf and the beauty of the course, and there are several books describing the history of the event. These include Clifford Roberts' *Story of the Augusta National Golf Club* (1976), Tom Flaherty's *The Masters* (1961), Dawson Taylor's *The Masters* (1973), Furman Bisher's *Augusta revisited* (1976) and Howard Liss's *The Masters tournament* (1974). This last title is not recommended, as it contains plenty of factual errors within its pages, but all the others have interest. Flaherty covers in detail the first 23 Masters tournaments, while Taylor's more up-to-date work waxes enthusiastic in a sub-title which reads "All about its history, its records, its players, its remarkable course and even more remarkable tournament". Julian May's *The Masters* (1975) describes the event for younger readers, and other authors — including Dick Schaap — give blow-by-blow accounts of particular championships. Schaap's *The Masters* is instant tape-recorded history, and describes the 1970 event.

This author uses the same technique for the United States Open in *Massacre at Winged Foot: the US Open minute by minute* (1974), while a more comprehensive coverage of the championship's history is given in Tom Flaherty's *The US Open, 1895-1965* (1966). For younger readers, there is Julian May's *US Open* (1975).

Dwayne Netland's *The Crosby: greatest show in golf* (1975) looks at the history of an event with strong show business connections which was originally established in 1937 by the singer and film star Bing Crosby, a keen and accomplished amateur golfer.

The major tournament in Britain, and indeed in Europe, is the Open Championship, which is the premier event in golf, if only because it has the longest history and strongest tradition of all major championships. Like the Masters, it has attracted a number of authors, starting in 1952 with Charles Mortimer and Fred Pignon, who looked at its first 90 years from 1860 to 1950 in their *Story of the Open Golf Championship* (1952). The tournament has, of course, been dealt with in many other general histories of the game, and Mortimer and Pignon include in their book two pages of bibliography giving further references. Tom Scott's *A century of golf (1860-1960)* (1960) briefly described the Championship's history in a pamphlet published by the Golf Foundation. Scott also joined forces with Geoffrey Cousins to produce a more considered volume, *A century of Opens* (1971). This book includes accounts of most of the most important Championships, and gives biographical information on winners of the event. More recently, two other books have appeared: Michael McDonnell's *Great moments in sport, golf* (1974), which covers the Open from 1934 to 1972, and Michael Hobbs's *Great Opens* (1976) sub-titled "Historic British and American championships, 1913-1975".

The matches played between Britain and the United States for the Ryder Cup seem to generate more interest in the United Kingdom than in the United States. This may well be firstly because in general the American players have little difficulty in winning this trophy, and secondly perhaps because there is considerably more interest in Britain in "head-to-head" match-play golf. Whatever the reason, there appears to be relatively few books published on this event, and two recent ones have both originated in Britain. Paul Trevillion's *Dead heat* (1969) is an interesting blow-by-blow account of the closest tie in the series, played in that year at Royal Birkdale in Lancashire. An earlier event which also caught the imagination of the British golfing public was the 1965 match, which was documented by Henry Longhurst and Geoffrey Cousins in their book *The Ryder Cup 1965* (1965).

The histories of golf in specific localities include some useful and very well written documents. Two of the key works on American golf are H.B. Martin's *Fifty years of American golf* (1936) and Herbert Warren Wind's *The story of American golf* (1948). Both are outstanding books by two of the best golfing writers. Martin's book was reprinted in its second edition format in 1966, and Wind's work continues to be updated, with a third edition published in 1975. The earliest separate book published on golf in the United States was *Golf in America* (1895), and although it is largely a practical manual on how to play its chief significance is probably its historical interest. Although it is over 85 years since this book was published, it seems to be reasonably available on the second-hand book market.

Golf appeared in Canada, with its strong British connections, somewhat earlier than in the United States, and a comprehensive *History of golf in Canada* was published by L.V. Kavanagh in 1973. An appendix to this book lists winners of all national and provincial championships in Canada up to that time. The history of golf in the Antipodes has been covered in Terry Smith's *Complete book of Australian golf* (1975) and two excellent volumes from a very small golf-playing nation, New Zealand. These are John Hornabrook's *The golden years of New Zealand golf* (1967) and *Golf in New Zealand: a centennial history* (1971) by G.M. Kelly. Although South Africa is now outside the British Commonwealth, its previous close associations with Britain are largely responsible for the popularity of golf in the republic. Paddy O'Donnell's *South Africa's wonderful world of golf* (1973) has valuable coverage of the game's history there.

Japanese golf has developed quite dramatically in post-war years, and an early paper describing its historical origins in that country appeared in English as far back as 1927. This was Chuzo Ito's brief paper 'Golf in Japan' which was published in *Japan Society Transactions* volume 24, 1927. This article discusses the establishment of the game in Japan in 1902, and mentions some of the problems in course construction in the early days. According to Ito, there were some 2,500 golfers in Japan by 1927.

Regional histories of the game have also been published, as well as many hundreds of histories of individual clubs. Two of the former worthy of mention are James Kelley's *Minnesota golf* (1976) and Jack Mahoney's *The golf history of New England* (1973). Of the club histories, pride of place must go to the Royal and Ancient at St Andrews and to the other early Scottish clubs. A number of books on the history of the town of St Andrews have included material on the golf club which it now recognises — along with its ancient university — as its most precious assets. Relationships between the town and the golf club have not always run smoothly, and these matters and others are related in these texts. Lyon's *History of St. Andrews* (1838) is a very early work which includes a chapter on the Royal and Ancient which at that time had been established for some 84 years. Much more recently James K. Robertson's *St. Andrews: home of golf* (1967) and Douglas Young's *St. Andrews: town and gown, Royal and Ancient* (1969) have greatly expanded knowledge on these relationships. Robertson's work was published locally and is a useful history of the game, while Young's work concentrates more on the town itself, though there are several chapters within it — notably numbers 7, 10 and 11 — which relate specifically to golf. Young's book details a "round of the modern Old course", while James Balfour's book *Reminiscences of golf on St. Andrews links* (1887) describes how it was played almost a hundred years ago.

The Royal and Ancient Club itself has had its history well documented, starting with H.S.C. Everard's 1907 work which was the first detailed treatise on the subject. The book was entitled *A history of the Royal and Ancient Golf Club, St. Andrews, 1754-1900*. A slim volume by Andrew Bennett, *The St. Andrews Golf Club centenary, 1843-1943* (1944), contained much interesting material about early artisan players and professionals in this part of Fife, but the next major work was J.B. Salmond's *Story of the R and A* in 1956. This book was written to commemorate the first 200 years of the club, and was supplemented in 1980 by Pat Ward-Thomas's excellent and readable *Royal and Ancient*, which was commissioned by the club and brings its history right up to the present day.

John Kerr's *Golf book of East Lothian* (1896) is widely recognised as the first of the golf club histories and a major historical sourcebook on the game. Other early works on Old Bruntsfield Links in Edinburgh, the Hawick Golf Club and the Glasgow Golf Club also appeared around the turn of the century. More recent Scottish club histories have included books on the Prestwick club, the Troon Golf Club, Melrose, Musselburgh, North Berwick, and even a remote smaller club at Stromness in the Orkney Islands. George Pottinger's *Muirfield and the Honourable Company* (1972) is deserving of special mention, as it relates the story of the Honourable Company of Edinburgh Golfers and their world-famous links at Muirfield on the Firth of Forth where many championships, including the Open, have been played.

English golf clubs also have their historical literature. These include J.H. Taylor's home club, the Royal North Devon at Westward Ho!, the Royal Liverpool at Hoylake in Cheshire and the Seaton Carew Golf Club in Durham among their number. Paul Macweeney's *Woodbrook Golf Club* (1976) covers the first 50 years of a leading Irish club and this seems to be one of the few texts written on clubs in that country. Eric Prain, the author of one of the key works in the instructional literature (see Chapter 3), wrote an interesting history of the Oxford and Cambridge Golfing Society from 1898 to 1948 which was published in 1949. Although society golf is an important element of the game, particularly in Britain, there seem to be relatively few volumes devoted exclusively to it. One exception is Robert Lapham's *Twenty years of life begins at forty* (1972) which tells of a unique golf tournament among friends in Texas.

American golf club histories include *St. Andrews (New York) Golf Club, 1888-1938* (1938) by H.B. Martin and A.B. Halliday, and Ford Frick's *This is St. Andrews* (1973), both of which tell the story of America's first golf club. Other substantial works have usually been published to celebrate either 50, or in a few cases 100 years, and one on the *Lakeside Golf Club of Hollywood* by professional writer Norman Blackburn ran to an amazing 344 pages. In Canada the Royal Montreal Golf Club produced a centennial volume in 1973, and the Toronto Club followed suit three years later in 1976. The Royal Sydney Golf Club in Australia, the Manawatu Golf Club in New Zealand, and the Pretoria Country Club in South Africa have all added to this sector of the literature, and although in some ways these are primarily for local consumption and of particular local interest to members and others it is a sector which shows signs of growth.

To complete this brief resume of the historical literature of golf it is appropriate to look at some more specialist volumes which are highly important in understanding the progress of the game. A fascinating report, *Rough and the fairway* which appeared in 1912, covered the economic and social aspects of caddying at that time. It is sub-titled "An enquiry by the Agenda Club into the golf caddie problem", and its contents throw much light on social attitudes of the period. Within the 163-page document there are chapters on demand and supply of caddies, on earnings and hours, on caddies and boy labour, and on methods of training regular caddies. Another important aspect of the game is the development of the rules and of handicapping. These are dealt with in Chapter 6 of this sourcebook, but two important contributions by C.B. Clapcott probably fit best in this section. These are *The history of handicapping* (1924), a brief ten-page pamphlet, and *The rules of the ten oldest golf clubs from 1754-1848* (1935). This latter book is the definitive study of the early rules of golf. Geoffrey Cousins in his *Golfers at law* (1958) also provides an excellent history of the rules of the game.

Finally, golfing equipment in its own right has not produced very many detailed historical studies, though there are many mentions in other compendia and general histories. A recent *tour-de-force* which helps to remedy this state of comparative neglect is Henderson and Stirk's *Golf in the making* (1979). This magnificent volume covers the history of golf up to 1914, and particularly concentrates on the development of the implements of the game. It includes much material selected from the British and United States patent literature, and in tapping these sources of information provides a unique and valuable reference work. The book also includes a brief chapter entitled 'A golf library' (pages 310-312) by H.R. Grant which mentions some of the more significant books published on the game of golf. The golf ball has its own history. J.S. Martin's *Curious history of the golf ball* (1968) is the first comprehensive study on this topic, and a short but useful bibliography is included. The book gains much from an excellent index. A much earlier pamphlet published by the Improved Golf Ball Company was a revised reprint of some articles originally appearing in the journal *Golfing*. This was *The evolution of the rubber-cored golf ball* (1904) written by C.T. Kingzett.

BIBLIOGRAPHY

ADAMSON, Alistair Beaton   In the wind's eye: North Berwick
    Golf Club.
        North Berwick, The author, 1980. A comprehensive history
        of the club from 1832 to date. North Berwick is the
        thirteenth oldest club in the game.

AGENDA CLUB   Rough and the fairway: an enquiry by the
    Agenda Club into the golf caddie problem.
        London, Heinemann, 1912. 163pp.

AITCHISON, Thomas C. *and* LORIMER, George
    Reminiscences of the Old Bruntsfield Links Golf Club,
    1866-1874.
        Edinburgh, The authors, 1902. 126pp. Includes many of the
        club lays (or poems) written to honour members on special
        occasions.

ALFANO, Pete   Grand slam.
    New York, Stadia Sports Publishing, 1973. 160pp.

BALFOUR, James   Reminiscences of golf on St. Andrews
    links.
        Edinburgh, David Douglas, 1887. 68pp. Descriptions of the
        Old Course and how it was played in the nineteenth century.

BARKOW, Al   Golf's golden grind: the history of the tour.
    New York, Harcourt Brace, 1974. 310pp.

BARRIE, James   Historical sketch of the Hawick Golf Club, with complete list of members, constitution and rules etc. appended.
Hawick, James Edgar, 1898. 183pp.

BARTNETT, Edmond P.   Seventy years of Wykagyl, 1898-1968.
New York, The club, 1968, 139pp.

BATTEN, Jack   Toronto Golf Club, 1876-1976.
Toronto, The club, 1976. 128pp.

BAUGHMAN, Ernest A.   How to caddie.
Chicago, Thomas, 1914.

BAYLESS, Don   Riviera's fifty golden years.
Los Angeles, The club, 1976. 108pp.

BEARDWOOD, Jack B.   History of the Los Angeles Country Club, 1898-1973.
Los Angeles, The club, 1973. 125pp.

BENNETT, Andrew   The St.Andrews Golf Club centenary, 1843-1943.
St. Andrews, W.C. Henderson, 1944. 75pp.

BISHER, Furman   Augusta revisited: an intimate view.
Birmingham, Al, Oxmoor House, 1976. 186pp. Covers the Masters tournament.

BLACKBURN, Norman   Lakeside Golf Club of Hollywood: fiftieth anniversary book.
Burbank, Ca., Cal-ad Co., 1975. 344pp.

BROWNING, Robert H.K.   A history of golf: the royal and ancient game.
London, Dent, 1955. 236pp. New York, Dutton.

— Super-golf.
London, Simpkin, Marshall etc., 1919. 144pp.

BUTTERFIELD Country Club, fiftieth anniversary, 1920-1970.
Hinsdale, Il, The club, 1970. 128pp.

CAMPBELL, Guy Colin.   Golf at Princes and Deal.
London, Newman Neame, 1950. 39pp. The history of two
famous English golf courses situated on the coast of Kent.

CARNEGIE, George Fullerton   Golfiana, or niceties connected
with the game of golf.
Edinburgh, J. Burnett, 1833. 8pp. Second edition Edinburgh,
Blackwood, 1833. 16pp. Third edition Edinburgh,
Blackwood, 1842. 26pp.

CLAPCOTT, C.B.   The history of handicapping.
(no imprint), 1924. 10pp.

— The rules of the ten oldest golf clubs from 1754-1848:
together with the rules of the Royal and Ancient Golf Club of
St. Andrews for the years 1858, 1877, 1888.
Edinburgh, *Golf Monthly*, 1935. 127pp.

CLARK, Robert   Golf: a royal and Ancient game.
Edinburgh, Clark, 1875. 285pp. Second edition, London,
Macmillan, 1893. Reprinted Wakefield, EP Publishing,
1975. 305pp. Boston, Charles River Books, 1976.

COLEBANK, Albert, *comp.*   A history of the Red Hill Country
Club.
Cucamonga, Ca, The club, 1972. 72pp.

COLVILLE, George M.   Five Open champions and the
Musselburgh golf story.
Edinburgh, Colville Books, 1980. A history of a famous links
in Scotland and of some of the famous players, such as Willie
Park, who played there.

COLVILLE, James   The Glasgow Golf Club, 1787-1907.
Glasgow, John Smith, 1907. 172pp. Includes much
interesting material about golf and golfers in the late
eighteenth and early nineteenth centuries.

COTTON, Henry   Golf: a pictorial history.
London, Collins, 1975. 240pp. Published in the United States
as A history of golf — illustrated. Philadelphia, Lippincott,
1975.

COUSINS, Geoffrey   Golf in Britain: a social history from
the beginning to the present day.
London, Routledge and Keen Paul, 1975. 176pp.

— Golfers at law.
London, S. Paul, 1958. 144pp. Complete history of the rules
of golf.
— Lords of the links: the story of professional golf.
London, Hutchinson, 1977. 176pp.
— *and* POTTINGER, Don   An atlas of golf.
London, Nelson, 1974. 96pp. A perceptive review of the
history of the game.
— *and* SCOTT, Tom   A century of Opens.
London, Muller, 1971. 232pp.

CRAWLEY, Leonard, *ed.*   Carling World Golf Championship,
Royal Birkdale Golf Club, Southport, Lancashire, England,
August 31-September 3, 1966: official programme and
souvenir.
London, Galizine, Chant, Russell, 1966. 124pp.

DARWIN, Bernard   British golf.
London, Collins, 1946. 47pp. (Britain in pictures series).

— Golf between the wars.
London, Chatto and Windus, 1944. 227pp.
— *and others.*   A history of golf in Britain.
London, Cassell, 1952. 312pp. Contributors to this volume
include H. Gardiner-Hill, Sir Guy Campbell, Henry Cotton,
Henry Longhurst, Leonard Crawley, Enid Wilson and Lord
Brabazon of Tara.

DRYSDALE, Alasdair M.   The Golf House Club, Elie: a
centenary history.
Elie, The club, 1975. 157pp.

DURKIN, Ted   The first fifty years, 1925-1975: Monterey
   Peninsula Country Club.
      Pebble Beach, Ca, The club, 1975. 127pp.

EDWARDS, Leslie   The Royal Liverpool Golf Club, 1869-
   1969: a short history of the club and of championships played
   over the Hoylake links.
      Liverpool, The club, 1969. 24pp.

[EKWANOK GOLF CLUB]   A history of Ekwanok:
   commemorating its seventy-fifth anniversary year.
      Manchester, Vt., The club, 1974. 64pp. One of the earliest
      American golf clubs.

EVANS, Webster   Rubs of the green: golf's triumphs and
   tragedies.
      London, Pelham, 1969. 157pp. Useful bibliography pp.149-
      150.

EVERARD, H.S.C.   A history of the Royal and Ancient Golf
   Club. St. Andrews, 1754-1900.
      Edinburgh, Blackwood, 1907. 306pp.

FARNIE, H.B.   The golfer's manual, by 'A Keen Hand': an
   historical and descriptive account of the national game of
   Scotland.
      Cupar, Whitehead and Orr, 1857. 84pp. Second edition.
      Cupar, Orr, 1862. Third edition. St. Andrews, Cook, 1870.
      Facsimile reprint London, Dropmore Press, 1947. 84pp.
      New York, Vantage Press, 1975.

FARRAR, Guy B.   The Royal Liverpool Golf Club: a history,
   1869-1932.
      Birkenhead, Willmer Bros., 1933. 310pp.

FITTIS, Robert Scott   Sports and pastimes of Scotland.
      Paisley, Gardner, 1891. 212pp.

FLAHERTY, Tom   The Masters: the story of golf's greatest
   tournament.
      New York, Holt, Rinehart and Winston, 1961. 150pp.

— The US Open, 1895-1965: the complete story of the United States Championship of Golf.
New York, E.P. Dutton, 1966. 224pp.

FORGAN, Robert   The golfer's handbook, including history of the game, hints to beginners, the feats of champion golfers, lists of leading clubs and their office bearers, etc.
Cupar, John Innes, Edinburgh, John Menzies and London, Marcus Ward, 1881. 83pp. Sixth edition 1897 retitled The golfer's manual.

FRICK, Ford   This is St. Andrews.
New York, The club, 1973. History of America's oldest golf club.

GALBRAITH, William   Prestwick St. Nicholas Golf Club.
Prestwick, The club, 1950. A history prepared for the club's centenary.

GIBSON, Nevin Herman   Great moments in golf.
New York, Barnes, and London, Yoseloff, 1973. 193pp. 193pp.

— A pictorial history of golf.
New York, Barnes, and London, Yoseloff, 1968. 237pp. A collection of superb golfing photographs. Second United States edition 1974.

GOODBAN, J.W.D. ed.   Royal North Devon Golf Club: a centenary anthology, 1864-1964.
Braunston, Devon, The club, 1963. 96pp.

GRAFFIS, Herb   The PGA: the official history of the Professional Golfers Association of America.
New York, Crowell, 1975. 559pp.

GRIMSLEY, Will   Golf: its history, people and events, with a special section by Robert Trent Jones.
Englewood Cliffs, NJ, Prentice Hall, 1966. 331pp. History of golf in the United States.

23

HARBOTTLE, George   The Northumberland Golf Club: a historical account of the first eighty years of the life of the club.
Newcastle-upon-Tyne, The club, 1978. 108pp.

HARPENDEN Golf Club, 1894-1954: diamond jubilee year souvenir handbook.
London, Golf Clubs Association, 1955. 40pp.

HECK, Phyllis Fraser, ed.   Dayton Country Club, 1876-1976.
Dayton, Ohio, The club, 1976. 144pp.

HENDERSON, Ian T. and STIRK, David   Golf in the making.
Bradford, Manningham Press for Henderson and Stirk Ltd., 1979. 332pp.

HEZLET, May   Ladies golf.
London, Hutchinson, 1904. 336pp. Second edition 1907.

HILTON, Harold H. and SMITH, Garden G.   The Royal and Ancient game of golf.
London, Golf Illustrated, 1912. 275pp.

HOBBS, Michael   Great Opens: historic British and American championships, 1913-1975.
Newton Abbot, David and Charles, 1976. 156pp. New York, Barnes, 1977.

HORNABROOK, John   The golden years of New Zealand golf.
Christchurch, NZ, Whitcomb and Tombs, 1967, 154pp.

HORNBY, Derek   The history of the Seaton Carew Golf Club, 1874-1974.
Hartlepool, The club, 1974. 108pp. One of the oldest English golf clubs.

HUTCHINSON, Horace G.   The book of golf and golfers.
London, Longmans Green, 1899. 316pp. Cheap edition 1900. Contributors include: Amy Pascoe, H.H. Hilton, J.H. Taylor, H.J. Whigham and Messrs. Sutton and Sons.

— Fifty years of golf.
London, Country Life, 1919. 229pp. New York, Charles
Scribners Sons.

— *ed.* Golf.
London, Longmans Green, 1890. 463pp. (The Badminton
library of sports and pastimes) Several later editions.

— Golfing.
London, Routledge, 1893. 120pp. (Oval series of games,
edited by C.W. Alcock). New York, E.P. Dutton. (A further
American edition was published in 1900 entitled Golf: a
complete history of the game) Second edition 1908.

ITO, Chuzo   "Golf in Japan" in *Japan Society Transactions*
volume 24, 1927, 56-62.

KAVANAGH, L.V.   The history of golf in Canada.
Toronto, Fitzhenry and Whiteside, 1973. 207pp.

KEANE, Christopher   The tour.
New York, Stein and Day, 1974. 237pp.

KELLEY, James E.   Minnesota golf: seventy five years of
tournament history.
Minneapolis, Minn, O.H. Dahlen, 1976. 288pp.

KELLY, G.M.   Golf in New Zealand: a centennial history.
Wellington, New Zealand Golf Association, 1971. 262pp.

KERR, John, *comp. and ed.*   The golf book of East Lothian.
London, Constable, 1896. 516pp.

KINGZETT, C.T.   The evolution of the rubber-cored golf ball.
London, Improved Golf Ball Co., 1904. 47pp.

KINNEY, H.A.   Brighton and Hove Golf Club, 1887-1973.
Brighton?, Commercial Printing and Stationery Co., 1974.
40pp.

KISSLING, John   Seventy years: a history of the Metropolitan
   Golf Club, Oakleigh, Victoria, which includes a history of the
   Caulfield Golf Club and a short account of early golf in Victoria,
   edited by Keith Brown.
   Melbourne, Macmillan, 1973. 156pp.

KLEIN, Dave   Great moments in golf.
   New York, Cawles Book Co., 1971. 128pp.

LAPHAM, Robert   Twenty years of life begins at
   forty: the story of a unique golf tournament.
   Harlingen, Texas, Fairway Publishing, 1972, 158pp.

LEACH, Henry   The spirit of the links.
   London, Methuen, 1907. 314pp. Philosophical
   thoughts on the game.

LEE, James P.   Golf in America: a practical manual.
   New York, Dodd Mead, 1895. 194pp.

LISS, Howard   The Masters tournament.
   New York, Dell, 1974. 219pp.

LONGHURST, Henry *and* COUSINS, Geoffrey   The Ryder
   Cup 1965.
   London, S. Paul, 1965. 64pp. + photographs.

LOW, John L.   Concerning golf, with a chapter on driving by
   Harold H. Hilton.
   London, Hodder and Stoughton, 1903. 217pp. Several later
   editions.

LYON, C.J.   The history of St. Andrews: ancient and modern.
   Edinburgh, Edinburgh Printing and Publishing Co., 1838.
   Updated and expanded edition in two volumes published in
   1843.

McCORMACK, Mark H.   The wonderful world of professional
   golf. New York, Atheneum Press, 1973. 467pp.

McDIARMID, D.J.   1876-1976: one hundred years of golf at
   Machrihanish.
   Machrihanish, The club, 1976. 52pp.

MacDONALD, Charles Blair   Scotland's gift — golf:
   reminiscences 1872-1927.
   New York, Charles Scribners Sons, 1928. 304pp.

McDONNELL, Michael   Great moments in sport, golf.
   London, Pelham, 1974. 200pp.

MACKENZIE, David A.   A history of the Melrose Golf
   Club.
   Melrose, The author, 1979. 137pp. Bibliography on page 137.

MACINTOSH, Ian M., *comp*   Troon Golf Club: its history
   from 1878.
   Troon, The club, 1974. 136pp.

MACWEENEY, Paul, *comp.*   Woodbrook Golf Club, fiftieth
   anniversary year, 1926-1976.
   Wicklow, The club, 1976.

MAHONEY, Jack   The golf history of New England.
   Wellesley, Maine, *New England Golf Magazine* 1973. 175pp.

MAIR, Lewine   The Dunlop lady golfer's companion
   Lavenham, Suffolk, Eastlands Press, 1980. 106pp.

MARSHALL, Keith Bernard   Golf galore.
   London, Kaye, 1960. 123pp. New York, Barnes, 1961.

MARTIN, H.B.   Fifty years of American golf.
   New York, Dodd Mead, 1936. 423pp. Second edition
   New York, Argosy-Antiquarian Ltd., 1966.

— The Garden City Golf Club (golden anniversary).
   Garden City, NY, The club, 1949. 67pp.

— *and* HALLIDAY, Alexander B.   St. Andrews (New York)
   Golf Club, 1888-1938.
   New York, The club, 1938. 146pp.

MARTIN, John Stuart   The curious history of the golf ball:
   mankind's most fascinating sphere.
   New York, Horizon Press, 1968. 192pp.

27

MAY, Julian   The Masters.
New York, Creative Education, 1975. (Sports classics series).
For younger readers.

— The PGA championship of golf.
New York, Creative Education, 1976. (Sports classics series).
For younger readers.

— The US Open.
New York, Creative Education, 1975. (Sports classics series).
For younger readers.

MILLER, Kenneth, E., *ed*.   Our first fifty years, 1922-1972.
Northbook, Il, Sunset Ridge Country Club, 1973. 62pp.

MORAN, Frank   Golfer's gallery.
Edinburgh, Oliver and Boyd, 1946. 196pp. Second edition
1949.

MORTIMER, Charles Gordon *and* PIGNON, Fred   Story of
the Open golf championship (1860-1950).
London, Jarrolds, 1952. 248pp.

NETLAND, Dwayne   The Crosby: greatest show in golf.
New York, Doubleday, 1975. 160pp.

NEW YORK TIMES   The complete book of golf: a New York
Times scrapbook history.
New York, *New York Times*, 1980. 208pp. Golf stories from
the newspaper 1895-1978.

ODELL, C.F.   History of the Pretoria Country Club.
Pretoria, The club, 1977. 168pp.

O'DONNELL, Paddy   South Africa's wonderful world of golf.
Cape Town, Don Nelson, 1973. 189pp.

PARK, Willie, Jr.   The game of golf.
London, Longmans Green, 1896. 277pp.

PATTERSON, A. Willing   The story of the Gulph Mills Golf
Club, 1916-1976.
Litits, Pa, Sutter House, 1976. 90pp.

POLLARD, Jack, *ed.*   Golf: the Australian way.
Melbourne, Lansdowne Press, 1970. 134pp. The instructional
material in this volume was previously published as The
secrets of Australian golfing success by Kel Nagle and
others. 1961. (*see* entry in Chapter 3).

POTTINGER, George   Muirfield and the Honourable Company.
Edinburgh, Scottish Academic Press, 1972. 146pp.

PRAIN, Eric M., *ed.*   The Oxford and Cambridge Golfing
Society, 1898-1948.
London, Eyre and Spottiswoode, 1949. 245pp.

PRICE, Charles   The world of golf: a panorama of six centuries
of the game's history.
New York, Random House, 1962. 307pp. London, Cassell,
1963. 320pp.

ROBERTS, Clifford   The story of the Augusta National Golf
Club.
New York, Doubleday, 1976. 255pp.

ROBERTSON, George Scott   A history of the Stromness golf
course: with notes on the Kirkwall and Isles courses.
Stromness, Orkney, The author, 1974. 19pp.

ROBERTSON, James Kinloch   St. Andrews: home of golf.
St. Andrews, Fife, Citizen Office, 1967. 173pp.

ROYAL ABERDEEN GOLF CLUB   Two hundred years of
golf, 1780-1980.
Aberdeen, The club, 1980. 148pp.

ROYAL MONTREAL GOLF CLUB   The Royal Montreal Golf
Club, 1873-1973: the centennial of golf in North America,
edited by Duncan C. Campbell.
Montreal, The club, 1973. 220pp.

ROYAL SYDNEY GOLF CLUB   A short history of the Royal
Sydney Golf Club.
Sydney, The club, 1949. 55pp. Leading Australian club
founded in 1893.

SALMOND, James Bell   The story of the R and A: being the
    history of the first 200 years of the Royal and Ancient Club of
    St. Andrews.
        London, Macmillan, 1956. 256pp. New York, St. Martins
        Press, 1956.

SCHAAP, Dick   Massacre at Winged Foot: the US Open,
    minute by minute.
        New York, Random House, 1974. 222pp.

— The Masters: the winning of a golf classic.
        New York, Random House, 1970. 235pp. London, Cassell,
        1971. 235pp.

SCOTT, Tom   A century of golf, (1860-1960)
        London, The Golf Foundation, 1960. 39pp.

— The Observer's book of golf.
        London, Warne, 1975. 192pp. (Observers pocket series)

— The story of golf from its origins to the present day.
        London, A. Barker, 1972. 166pp.

SEIFERT, H.A.   The first seventy five years of the Manawatu Golf
    Club, Palmerston North, New Zealand.
        Palmerston North, NZ, The club, 1970. 104pp.

SHAW, James E., *comp.*   Prestwick Golf Club: a history and
    some records.
        Glasgow, Jackson, Son and Co., 1938. 143pp. Handsomely
        produced club history.

SIMPSON, Walter G.   The art of golf.
        Edinburgh?, Hamilton, 1887. Second edition Edinburgh,
        David Douglas, 1892. 186pp.

SMITH, Charles   Aberdeen golfers: records and reminiscences.
        London, The author, 1909. 167pp.

SMITH, Garden G.   The world of golf.
        London, A.D. Innes, 1898. 330pp. (The Isthmian Library
        no. 3).

SMITH, Terry   The complete book of Australian golf.
North Sydney, Jack Pollard, 1975. 229pp.

STEWART, James Lindsey, *ed*.   Golfiana miscellanea, being a
collection of interesting monographs on the royal and ancient
game of golf.
London, Hamilton Adams, 1887. 300pp.

TAYLOR, Arthur V., *ed*.   Originaes golfianae: the birth of golf
and its early childhood as revealed in a chance-discovered
manuscript from a Scottish monastery.
Woodstock, Vt, Elm Tree Press, 1912. 58pp.

TAYLOR, Dawson   The Masters: all about its history, its records,
its players, its remarkable course and even more remarkable
tournament.
Second edition, revised, New York, Barnes and London,
Yoseloff, 1973. 159pp.

— St. Andrews: cradle of golf.
New York, Barnes and London, Yoseloff, 1976. 207pp.
History of the Old Course up to 1976. Bibliography on pp.
202-203.

TAYLOR, J.H.   Taylor on golf: impressions, comments and
hints.
London, Hutchinson, 1902. 328pp. New York, Appleton.

THOMAS, Ivor S.   Formby Golf Club, 1884-1972.
Formby, The club, 1973. 186pp.

TREVILLION, Paul   Dead heat: the '69 Ryder Cup classic.
London, S. Paul, 1969. 128pp.

WARD-THOMAS, Pat   The Royal and Ancient.
Edinburgh, Scottish Academic Press for the Royal and
Ancient Golf Club of St. Andrews, 1980. 124pp.

WEEKS, Edward, *comp. and ed*.   Myopia: a centennial
chronicle, 1875-1975.
Hamilton, Ma, The club, 1975. 151pp.

WETHERED, Joyce *and others*   The game of golf.
London, Seeley Service, 1931. 251pp. (The Lonsdale Library
volume). Philadelphia, Lippincott, 1931. Second United
States edition New York, Barnes, 1951. Includes sections by
Joyce and Roger Wethered, Bernard Darwin, Horace G.
Hutchinson and T.C. Simpson.

WILSON, Enid   A gallery of women golfers.
London, *Country Life*, 1961. 192pp.

WIND, Herbert Warren   The story of American golf: its
champions and its championships.
New York, Farrar and Strauss, 1948. 502pp. Second edition.
New York, Simon and Schuster, 1956. 564pp. (This edition
reprinted Westport, Ct, Greenwood Press, 1972) Third
edition New York A. Knopf, 1975.

YOUNG, Douglas C.C.   St. Andrews: town and gown, Royal
and Ancient.
London, Cassell, 1969. 276pp. An excellent book which
covers three major facets of Scottish life, learning, religion
and golf.

CHAPTER TWO

THE
GOLFERS

As in all aspects of human endeavour it is the individuals concerned in the activity who create most interest. The previous chapter covered the historical aspects of the game of golf, and it is, of course, both difficult and perhaps undesirable to try to separate personal histories and reminiscences from the historical mainstream. Nevertheless, if only because of the number of publications, a separate, but closely related, chapter does seem appropriate. Those seeking information on outstanding players of the game and on others who have some particularly significant or interesting contribution to make to golf, should find this separate chapter of value.

There is also a close link with succeeding sections of this work. In the next chapter, where the vast amount of documentation on "how-to-play" is discussed, there are many examples of books which are basically instructional which also include sections of varying length on the life story of the writer of the manual. The fourth chapter also includes many biographical sketches within the anthologies and collections of essays which make up a large part of it, and even some of the fictional entries are thinly-veiled biographies. With these reminders of the diversity of this sector, the preamble to this chapter can be completed by reminding the user that the detailed indexes provided will identify all named individuals discussed, no matter which chapter they are primarily assigned to.

One of the earliest works which might properly be labelled collected biography is J. Gordon McPherson's *Golf and golfers, past and present* (1891). This was published in the home country of golf at Edinburgh. In 1907 Henry Leach's *Great golfers in the making* consisted of autobiographical sketches of the most celebrated players of the previous 50 years. Both amateurs and professionals were represented, and a list of their names provides a roll call of leading exponents from Scotland and England up to that time. Legendary players like J.E. Laidlay and Harold Hilton among the amateurs and the "immortal triumvirate" of J.H. Taylor, Harry Vardon and James Braid of the professional ranks are all included. This substantial volume of almost 300 pages has an index which adds greatly to its usefulness. In rather more recent times the American writer H.B. Martin's *Great golfers in the making* was published on both sides of the Atlantic in 1932. Within the past 20 years, and more easily available in consequence, there have been a number of significant works of this genre, including Pat Ward-Thomas's *Masters of golf* (1961) and Scott and Cousins's *Golf secrets of the masters* (1968). This latter volume appeared in the United States in the following year entitled *The golf immortals* with a substantially altered text presumably to increase its appeal to the American market. The British journalist Ronald Heager in *Kings of clubs* (1968) discusses 16 golfers who are not all world class players but nevertheless represent the many facets of the golfing world. *Golf: the great ones* (1971) by Michael McDonnell includes chapters on Vardon, Henry Cotton, Peter Thomson and some of the top American players such as Bobby Jones, Ben Hogan, Arnold Palmer and Jack Nicklaus. A somewhat similar volume, *Golf to remember* (1978) by Michael Hobbs and Peter Alliss, also looks at the individual performances of some of these (and other) golfers, while *Superstars of golf* (1978) by Nick Seitz profiles Nicklaus, Raymond Floyd, Johnny Miller and others in the top flight of the professional ranks. Rex Lardner's book *Great golfers* (1970) offers biographical sketches of famous American golfers and is aimed at younger readers. As can be seen, the titles of most of these books show little originality, and this also has to be said for Ross Goodner's *Golf's greatest* (1978) which includes brief biographies of the 35 players who, up to that time, had been selected for inclusion in the World Golf Hall of Fame in Pinehurst, North Carolina. Biographical dictionaries and who's who's are discussed in Chapter 6 among other general reference works.

Most of those interested in the game have their own favourites for the all-time great players and any selection made for the purposes of this publication must, to some extent, reflect a personal choice even if largely based on an analysis of the documents available. Few, however, would argue with the inclusion of

Robert Tyre "Bobby" Jones, Jr., since his playing achievements and subsequent contributions as a teacher and promoter of the game are widely known. Jones dominated the game in the late 1920s and early 1930s, winning all the major tournaments of the time including the so-called "grand slam", including amateur and open championships. Jones's prowess is particularly well documented since he was fortunate to have his own "Boswell" in Oscar Bane Keeler who travelled with him to all his major tournaments throughout his playing career. Keeler assisted Jones with *Down the fairway* (first edition 1927) in which he described the earlier part of his career. This book ran to several editions. Keeler also wrote *The boy's life of Bobby Jones* (1931) and in 1955 Grantland Rice edited *The Bobby Jones story* from the writings of Keeler. Jones himself produced an autobiography, *Golf is my game* (1960) which also included a section of golf instruction; and in 1980 Dick Miller's *Triumphant journey: the saga of Bobby Jones and the grand slam of golf* was conceived as a 50th anniversary tribute.

Another quite different golfer, who had a tremendous influence on the game's progress in the post-World War II years, is Arnold Palmer. Palmer's charisma and approach to the game caught the imagination of the American public and caused a tremendous upsurge in the popularity of the sport as a spectacle. Palmer was also a smart business man who, with the aid of Mark H. McCormack, exploited many of the lucrative opportunities for endorsement of equipment and clothing. At least three biographies and two autobiographies are available to chart Palmer's progress throughout his career. His own work *Portrait of a professional golfer* appeared in 1964 and was followed by *Arnie: evolution of a legend* (1967) by manager McCormack as part of the super public relations campaign to promote the professional golf circuit. A more objective and straightforward account of Palmer's rise to fame comes in *Arnold Palmer* (1967) by the leading magazine *Golf Digest*, while in 1972 Furman Bisher and Murray Olderman's *The birth of a legend* looked back with a well-written account of 1960, the year in which Palmer burst into full prominence. *Go for broke*, the title of Palmer's second autobiographical volume, written in collaboration with W.B. Furlong in 1973, succinctly describes the philosophy he adopts on the golf course — a philosophy which endeared him to the supporters and kept them following his progress long after he had passed his peak.

The player who overtook Palmer and dominated world professional golf for the next decade and more was Jack Nicklaus.

Nicklaus has won more major championships than any previous player, and his life is documented, at an early stage, in *The greatest game of all* (1969), in which his co-author is the great American golfing writer Herbert Warren Wind; and more recently in a pictorial autobiography entitled *On and off the fairway* (1980) written with Ken Bowden.

Earlier American golfing "greats" include Ben Hogan, who won 68 major tournaments and has been claimed by some as the greatest golfer of all time. Gene Gregston's unauthorised biography *Ben Hogan: the man who played for glory* was published in 1978. Another biography, *My partner, Ben Hogan* (1954), was written by leading American professional Jimmy Demaret, who was himself a pioneer of the United States professional tour. Walter Hagen was fortunate in his choice of co-author, and the resulting book, *The Walter Hagen story* (1956), is interesting and well written. It describes his career in the 1920s and 1930s and shows that his influence on the development of professional golf was considerable. Finally in this group of leading American players Sam Snead has to be included. Snead was virtually a self-taught player who became one of the best players of all time. His book *The education of a golfer* (1962) covers his career, which spanned five decades.

Tom Morris was a Scottish golfing legend of the last century, and W.W. Tulloch's *Life of Tom Morris* catches the flavour of the man and his period. The book is subtitled "With glimpses of St. Andrews and its golfing celebrities". Another Scottish hero was James Braid who is fortunate indeed to have Bernard Darwin as his biographer. Braid was a great champion whose influence was significant in improving the image of the professional golfer in Great Britain. Darwin's *James Braid* (1952) is a warm and appreciative story of Braid's playing career, his career as a golf course architect, and of his personal life.

J.H. Taylor was a Devon man and a contemporary of Braid and of Harry Vardon. His book *Golf my life's work* (1943) describes many early developments including the artisan golfers movement, public course development, and the growth of the Professional Golfers' Association. The third member of the triumvirate, Harry Vardon, was born in the Channel Islands and won the Open Championship no fewer than six times. Vardon's first book, *The complete golfer* (1905), is aptly titled; it is partly instructional and partly early reminiscences. The book ran to several later editions and was reprinted most recently in 1977. Vardon also had a high reputation in the United States and is generally regarded as one of the greatest players of all time. He published a more comprehensive autobiography, *My golfing life,* in 1933.

Another leading British golfer, Thomas Henry Cotton, has contributed much to golf both as a player and as a teacher. As will be seen from other chapters of this book, Cotton has also been a prolific author of books on the game. *Thanks for the game* (1980) is a mixture of tips and reminiscences based on a long career which started in the late 1920s. This career took him to several wins in the Open and to his later work as a golf course designer, teacher and broadcaster on golf. Tony Jacklin, in 1969 and 1970, did much for British golfing prestige when, for a time, he was holder of both the United States and British Open championships. He told his own story to that point in his career in *Jacklin: the champion's own story* (1970). In 1979 a golfing journalist, Liz Kahn, produced *Tony Jacklin: the price of success* (1979) which analyses both his early successes and the later 1970s when his fortunes were at a lower ebb.

Gary Player has had a lengthy and highly successful career, winning all the major tournaments including three Masters and three Opens. The South African's *Grand slam golf* (1966) gave some indications of Player's determination to succeed and his willingness to work incredibly hard to achieve that success. In *Gary Player, world golfer* (1974), written in collaboration with Floyd Thatcher, Player updates his life story in somewhat greater depth.

There are many other tournament professionals who have achieved varying degrees of success and have turned to the written word. Although the golfing public is always more interested in the big names many of these less successful players have much of interest to communicate, and those seeking hard information on many aspects of the game are well advised to look in this direction. One such author is Peter Alliss whose playing career, though successful, was probably less influential than his later work as a commentator on, and populariser of, the game. Alliss was the son of a famous golfing father — who also wrote about the game (see Chapter 3) — and his several golfing books include *Alliss through the looking glass* (1963). Other British professionals who have added to this sector of the literature include Eric Brown, one-time Ryder Cup captain; Dai Rees, who also led the British team several times in this event; Neil Coles, who has had considerable success on the British and European circuit; and the much younger Nick

Faldo, whose biography *The rough with the smooth* (1980) was greeted by some reviewers as "rather premature".

Golfers of a much earlier generation are represented by Sandy Herd's *My golfing life* (1923), Andrew Kirkaldy's *Fifty years of golf: my memories* (1921) and George Duncan's *Golf at the gallop* (1951). Part two of the last-named is instructional material. Many leading American professionals, sometimes with the aid of "ghost" writers, have also written lucid and valuable texts. These include Frank Beard, whose book *Pro* (1970) offered an authentic inside view of the United States professional tour. Gene Sarazen's *Thirty years of championship golf* (1950), jointly authored by Herbert Warren Wind, is an excellent biography of a very great player. Other interesting, and sometimes colourful, accounts of life on the "tour" include Tommy Bolt's *The hole truth* (1971), Dave Hill's *Teed off* (1977) and *Tony Lema's inside story of the professional golf tour* (1964), which was published shortly before the author's untimely death in an air crash. In similar vein are Gene Littler's *The real score* (1976) and Doug Sanders' *Come swing with me* (1974). Sanders has a colourful life style, both on and off the golf course, but is best remembered in Britain (somewhat unfortunately) for missing a four-foot putt which cost him victory in the Open Championship of 1970. An excellent biography from an earlier era is Horton Smith's *The velvet touch* (1965). Smith's career spanned the years from hickory to steel-shafted clubs and he won tournaments with both. Smith was noted as a marvellous putter, and produced a book on this topic which is listed in the next chapter. Several biographies aimed at younger readers complete this section. They include *Johnny Miller* (1975) by Sam Hasegawn and *Supermex: the Lee Trevino story* (1973) by Robert B. Jackson.

Gary Player, as noted above, has done much for South African golf, and in the years immediately prior to his ascendancy another splendid golfer emerged from this part of the world. His name was Bobby Locke and he won the British Open several times in the period immediately after World War II. Locke's own book, *Bobby Locke on golf* (1953), is partly autobiographical and partly instructional, while *King of the links* (1954) by Ronald Norval describes his playing career in some detail. Australia has also produced world-class golfers, and two who were particularly successful in the 1950s were Norman von Nida and Peter Thomson. Thomson's *The wonderful world of golf* (1969) is an entertaining book on his very successful career which included winning the

39

Open Championship five times. Von Nida's *Golf is my business* (1956) tells of the author's golfing progress at around the same period.

Though the professionals tend to dominate the present-day game many amateurs have had extremely successful playing careers and, in many cases, have contributed much to the administration of the game as well. Jerome D. Travers, a leading American amateur, certainly comes into this category, and his book *The fifth estate* (1926) is of considerable interest because of this. Another leading American was Francis Ouimet, who eventually became the first American captain of the Royal and Ancient at St Andrews. Ouimet's reminiscences, *A game of golf* (1932), were written much earlier in his distinguished career. Leading British amateur players like Harold H. Hilton set down their reminiscences as long ago as 1907. Hilton's book *My golfing reminiscences* conveys much of the flavour of the keen rivalry between the professionals and the amateurs in these times. Freddie Tait was an exceptionally gifted player who was killed in the South African War in 1900. In that year John L. Low's *F.G. Tait: a record, being his life, letters and golfing diary* was published. In much more recent times P.B. "Laddie" Lucas has published his reflections under the title of *The sport of princes* (1980). Other amateur players, who were more distinguished for their work off the golf course but nevertheless loved the game, include the world-famous nuclear scientist Lord Rutherford of Nelson. A brief 33-page memoir by Frederick George Mann tells of Rutherford's devotion to golf. The pamphlet is entitled *Lord Rutherford and the golf course* (1976). In a quite different vein is Charles Boswell's *Now I see* (1969), which describes how Boswell, a blinded war veteran, took up golf as therapy.

The women's game has also produced some fine players some of whom have emerged as good teachers of the game, and a few as readable authors. An early book by Mabel Stringer entitled *Golfing reminiscences* (1924) traced the development of the women's game from the 1890s. A leading American lady golfer, Glenna Collett, did much to develop the women's game, and her book *Ladies in the rough* (1928) tells of the earlier part of her golfing career. In the early 1930s two significant books appeared in Britain. The first was by Eleanor E. Helme, a leading player of the time, who also wrote a number of very useful "how to play" books. Her autobiography *After the ball* (1931) was subtitled "Merry memoirs of a golfer, being the story of 46 championships and other golfing occasions pursued with club, notebook and pencil", and reflects her interest in, and contributions to, golfing journalism. Joyce Wethered's *Golfing memories and methods* (1933) is a major work, since Miss Wethered had an almost faultless technique and, both by example and by the later work she did in administration of the game, was the single most important influence on the development of women's golf, in Britain at least.

On the other side of the Atlantic there have been few women golfers better than Mildred "Babe" Zaharias, who was a leading athlete before taking up golf and mastering that game. Mrs Zaharias' own life story, *This life I've led*, appeared in 1956 just as her terminal illness had been diagnosed. Her brave fight against cancer, and her whole sporting career, are well documented in an excellent biography, *Whatta girl: the Babe Didrikson story* (1977) by W.O. Johnson and N.P. Williamson. Current leading players on the Ladies Professional Golf Association (LPGA) tournament circuit include Nancy Lopez and Jane Blalock. Lopez' life story, to the age of 24, is told in *The education of a woman golfer* (1979) after two years in which she dominated the LPGA tour. Blalock's *The guts to win* (1977) documents the growth of the women's professional game over the previous decade. Laura Baugh has had two books written about her, and both are for younger readers. They are *Laura Baugh: golf's golden girl* (1974) by Linda Jacobs and *Laura Baugh* (1976) by Mary J. O'Hara and John Keely. Ms. Baugh's attractions are not only because of her golfing prowess, and although she has not been particularly successful in the playing sense she has done much to "glamorize" and make popular the women's tour.

Last — but by no means least — there are the biographies of the golf writers, of caddie-masters, and of golf promoters and golf agents. There are no better examples of good creative writing in the literature than the autobiographical trilogy by Bernard Darwin. The first volume, *Green memories,* appeared in 1928 when Darwin had already been writing about golf in the London *Times* and elsewhere for two decades. *Life is sweet, brother* (1940) was the second volume, written in the early part of World War II, and *The world that Fred made* (1955) completed the set.

Darwin set new standards for golf reporting, and was a prolific author on many aspects of the game. Following closely in this tradition, Henry Longhurst had a varied career — including briefly a period as a Member of Parliament. In his later years he became known to a very wide audience through his television commentaries and his regular column in the London *Sunday Times*. His first volume of autobiography was *It was good while it lasted* (1941) with a second edition in 1945, and *My life and soft times* (1971) was published a few years before he died. Another leading golf correspondent with a wide reputation is Peter Dobereiner, who writes regularly for the *Observer* newspaper in London and for the American monthly journal *Golf Digest*. Dobereiner's *The game with the hole in it* (1970) is an amusing and discursive account of many aspects of the game.

Exposure on television has even brought widespread fame to the caddies of the top players, and Angelo Argea's memoirs *The bear and I* describe life on the tournament circuit with Jack Nicklaus. Another unique book is James Sheridan's *Sheridan of Sunningdale* (1967), which looks at golf through the very different eyes of a man who spent 56 years as a caddie-master at a major golf club. Fred Corcoran's *Unplayable lies* (1965) is the autobiography of a leading golf promoter and manager of some of the leading players, while Bucky Way's *Sign 'em up, Bucky* (1975) is subtitled "The adventures of a sport agent" and is largely devoted to the author's involvement with Lee Trevino.

BIBLIOGRAPHY

COLLECTED BIOGRAPHY

BROWN, Eric *and* HERRON, Allan   Out of the bag.
   London, S. Paul, 1964. 159pp. Anecdotes on contemporary
   players.

DARSIE, Darsie L.   ● My greatest day in golf with contributions by Arthur J. Lacey.
   New York, A.S. Barnes, 1950. 210pp. London, Redman,
   1952. 254pp. 51 famous golfers reminisce about their most
   memorable round.

GLEASON, Dan   The great, the grand and the also-ran: rabbits
   and champions on the pro golf tour.
   New York, Random House, 1976. 238pp.

GOODNER, Ross   Golf's greatest: the legendary World Golf
   Hall of Famers.
   New York, Simon and Schuster, 1978. 240pp.

HEAGER, Ronald   Kings of clubs.
   London, S. Paul, 1968. 159pp.

HOBBS, Michael *and* ALLISS, Peter   Golf to remember.
   London, Batsford and New York, Doubleday,
   1978. 168pp. Looks at the performances of some of the
   world's great players from Taylor and Vardon to Nicklaus,
   Miller, Player, Jacklin and Watson.

43

KLEIN, Dave   Golf's big three.
New York, Stadia Sports Publishers, 1973. (Collectors item series)

LARDNER, Rex   Great golfers.
New York, Putnam, 1970. 160pp. (Sports shelf series) For younger readers.

LEACH, Henry, *ed.*   Great golfers in the making: being autobiographical accounts of the early progress of the most celebrated players, with reflections on the morals of their experience by John L. Low, Harold H. Hilton, Horace G. Hutchinson, J.E. Laidlay, Walter J. Travis, James Robb, Edward Blackwell, Harry Vardon, James Braid, J.H. Taylor, Alexander Herd, Willie Park, Tom Morris, Jack White etc. etc.
London, Methuen, 1907. 299pp.

McDONNELL, Michael   Golf: the great ones.
London, Pelham, 1971. 147pp.

McPHERSON, J. Gordon   Golf and golfers, past and present.
Edinburgh, Blackwood, 1891. 100pp.

MARTIN, Harry Brownlaw   Great golfers in the making.
New York, Dodd Mead and London, John Lane, 1932. 268pp.

SCOTT, Tom *and* COUSINS, Geoffrey   Golf secrets of the masters.
London, S. Paul, 1968. 136pp. United States edition entitled The golf immortals. New York, Hart, 1969. This edition is substantially different to the British edition.

SEITZ, Nick   Superstars of golf.
New York, Simon and Schuster, 1978. 192pp.

VAN RIPER, Guernsey   Golfing greats: two top pros.
New Canaan, Garrard, 1975.

WARD-THOMAS, Pat   Masters of golf.
London, Heinemann, 1961. 257pp.

INDIVIDUAL BIOGRAPHY

ALLISS, Peter
ALLISS, Peter *and* FERRIER, Bob   Alliss through the looking
   glass: my world of golf.
      London, Cassell, 1963. 300pp.

ARGEA, Angelo
ARGEA, Angelo *and* EDMONDSON, Jolee   The bear and I.
   New York, Atheneum Press, 1979. 192pp.

BAUGH, Laura
JACOBS, Linda   Laura Baugh: golf's golden girl.
      St Paul, Minn, EMC Corporation, 1974. (Women who win
      series no. 2)

O'HARA, Mary J. *and* KEELY, John   Laura Baugh.
      New York, Creative Education, 1976. (Sports superstars
      series) For younger readers.

BEARD, Frank
BEARD, Frank   Pro: Frank Beard on the golf tour, edited by
   Dick Schaap.
      New York, World Publishing Co., 1970. 323pp.

BLALOCK, Jane
BLALOCK, Jane *and* NETLAND, Dwayne   The guts to win.
      New York, Simon and Schuster, 1977. 158pp. Listed in some
      sources as 'Drive to win'.

BOLT, Tommy
BOLT, Tommy *and* MANN, Jimmy   The hole truth: inside big-
   time, big-money golf.
      Philadelphia, Lippincott, 1971. 187pp. Biography of one of
      the more colourful golfers on the tour. Bolt won the United
      States Open Championship and many other tournaments.

BOSWELL, Charles
BOSWELL, Charles *and* ANDERS, Curt   Now I see.
      New York, Meredith Press, 1969. 208pp.

BRAID, James
DARWIN, Bernard   James Braid.
    London, Hodder and Stoughton, 1952. 196pp.

BROWN, Eric
BROWN, Eric   Knave of clubs.
    London, S. Paul, 1961. 158pp.

CASPER, Billy
PEERY, Paul D.   Billy Casper: winner.
    Englewood Cliffs, NJ, Prentice-Hall, 1969. 207pp. Story
    of leading American professional.

COLES, Neil
COLES, Neil   Neil Coles on golf.
    London, S. Paul, 1965. 125pp. Coles is a leading British
    tournament professional.

COLLETT, Glenna
COLLETT, Glenna *and* NEVILLE, James M.   Ladies in the
    rough.
    New York, A.A. Knopf, 1928. 208pp.

CORCORAN, Fred
CORCORAN, Fred *and* HARVEY, Bud   Unplayable lies.
    New York, Duell, Sloan and Pearce, 1965. 274pp.

COTTON, Henry
COTTON, Henry   Thanks for the game: the best of golf with
    Henry Cotton.
    London, Sidgwick and Jackson, 1980. 176pp.

DALY, Fred
McQUILLAN, Eoin   The Fred Daly story.
    Belfast, Blackstaff Press, 1978. 132pp. Story of leading Irish
    professional golfers who won the Open Championship in
    1947.

DARWIN, Bernard
DARWIN, Bernard   Green memories.
    London, Hodder and Stoughton, 1928. 332pp.

— Life is sweet, brother.
London, Collins, 1940. 285pp.

— The world that Fred made: an autobiography.
London, Chatto and Windus, 1955. 256pp.

DIDRIKSON, Mildred   see *ZAHARIAS, Mildred Didrikson*

DOBEREINER, Peter
DOBEREINER, Peter   The game with the hole in it.
London, Faber, 1970. 142pp.

DUNCAN, George
DUNCAN, George   Golf at the gallop, edited by Edgar Turner.
London, Sporting Handbooks, 1951. 192pp.

ELDER, Lee
JACOBS, Linda   Lee Elder: the daring dream.
St Paul, Minn, EMC Corporation, 1976. (Black American athletes series) Life story, for younger readers, of one of the few black Americans to make the "big time" in professional golf.

FALDO, Nick
FALDO, Nick *and* PRATT, Mitchell   The rough with the smooth: breaking into professional golf.
London, S. Paul, 1980. 192pp.

GREGSON, Malcolm
GREGSON, Malcolm   Golf with Gregson.
London, S. Paul, 1968. 127pp. Story of British professional player whose best years were in the late 1960s.

HAGEN, Walter
HAGEN, Walter *and* HECK, Margaret Seaton   The Walter Hagen story.
New York, Simon and Schuster, 1956. 342pp. London, Heinemann, 1957. 299pp.

HARRIS, Robert
HARRIS, Robert   Sixty years of golf.
London, Batchworth Press, 1953. 131pp. Story of a one-time British amateur champion and Walker Cup player.

47

HELME, Eleanor E.
HELME, Eleanor E.   After the ball: merry memoirs of a golfer, being the story of 46 championships and other golfing occasions pursued with club, notebook and pencil.
London, Hurst and Blackett, 1931. 320pp.

HERD, Alexander
HERD, Sandy *and* FOSTER, Clyde   My golfing life.
London, Chapman and Hall, 1923. 246pp.

HILL, Dave
HILL, Dave *and* SEITZ, Nick   Teed off: a candid probing book about the tour by golf's most controversial player.
Englewood Cliffs, N J, Prentice-Hall, 1977. 228pp.

HILTON, Harold H.
HILTON, Harold H.   My golfing reminiscences.
London, James Nisbet, 1907. 247pp.

HITCHCOCK, Jimmy
HITCHCOCK, Jimmy   Master golfer.
London, S. Paul, 1967. 192pp. Story of leading British professional golfer.

HOGAN, Ben
DEMARET, Jimmy   My partner, Ben Hogan.
New York, McGraw-Hill and London, P. Davies, 1954. 215pp. London, Hamilton, 1957. 187pp. (Paperback edition)

GREGSTON, Gene   Ben Hogan: the man who played for glory.
Englewood Cliffs, N J, Prentice-Hall, 1978. 256pp. London, Pelham, 1980. 192pp.

JACKLIN, Tony
JACKLIN, Tony   Jacklin: the champion's own story.
London, Hodder and Stoughton, 1970. 192pp. New York, Simon and Schuster, 1970.

KAHN, Liz   Tony Jacklin: the price of success.
London, Hamlyn, 1979. 160pp.

JONES, Robert Tyre "Bobby"
JONES, Bobby   Golf is my game.
>New York, Doubleday, 1960. 255pp. London, Chatto and
>Windus, 1961. 270pp.

— *and* KEELER, Oscar Bane   Down the fairway: the golf life
and play of Robert T. Jones, Jr.
>New York, Minton Balch, 1927. London, Allen and Unwin,
>1927. 240pp.

— The Bobby Jones story: from the writings of O.B. Keeler, edited
by Grantland Rice.
>London, Foulsham for the Fireside Press, 1955. 304pp.

MILLER, Dick   Triumphant journey: the saga of Bobby Jones
and the grand slam of golf.
>New York, Holt, Rinehart and Winston, 1980. 240pp.

KEELER, Oscar Bane
KEELER, Oscar Bane   The autobiography of an average golfer.
>New York, Greenberg, 1925. 247pp.

KIRKALDY, Andrew
KIRKALDY, Andrew *and* FOSTER, Clyde   Fifty years of golf:
my memories.
>London, Unwin, 1921. 224pp.

KIRKWOOD, Joe
KIRKWOOD, Joe *and* FAY, Barbara   The links of life.
>[no imprint] , 1973. 141pp. Biography of a famous trick shot
>player.

LEMA, Tony
LEMA, Tony *and* BROWN, Gwilym S.   Tony Lema's inside
story of the professional golf tour.
>London, Foulsham, 1964. 191pp. Originally published as
>Golfer's gold: an inside view of the pro tour. Boston, Little
>Brown, 1964. 248pp.

LITTLER, Gene
LITTLER, Gene *and* TOBIN, Jack   The real score.
>Waco, Texas, Word Books, 1976. 199pp.

LOCKE, Arthur D.Arcy "Bobby"
LOCKE, Bobby   Bobby Locke on golf.
    London, *Country Life,* 1953. 196pp. New York, Simon and
    Schuster, 1954.

NORVAL, Ronald   King of the links: the story of Bobby
    Locke.
    Cape Town, Maskew Miller, 1954. London, Bailey and
    Swinfen, 1954. 108pp.

LONGHURST, Henry
LONGHURST, Henry   It was good while it lasted.
    London, Dent, 1941. 192pp. Second edition 1945.

— My life and soft times.
    London, Cassell, 1971. 366pp.

LOPEZ, Nancy
LOPEZ, Nancy *and* SCHWED, Peter   The education of a
    woman golfer.
    New York, Simon and Schuster, 1979. 160pp. London,
    Pelham, 1980.

LUCAS, P.B. "Laddie"
LUCAS, P.B.   The sport of princes: reflections of a golfer.
    London, S. Paul, 1980. 192pp.

MILLER, Johnny
HASEGAWN, Sam   Johnny Miller.
    New York, Creative Education, 1975. Miller is a leading
    American professional who won many major tournaments
    in the mid-1970s. For younger readers.

MOODY, Orville
MOODY, Orville *and* HISKEY, Jim   Golf how by Orville who?
    New York, Hawthorn, 1971. 199pp. Moody won the United
    States Open Championship in 1969.

MORRIS, Tom
TULLOCH, W.W.   Life of Tom Morris: with glimpses of St.
    Andrews and its golfing celebrities.
    London, Werner Laurie, 1907. 334pp.

NICKLAUS, Jack
NICKLAUS, Jack *and* BOWDEN, Ken   On and off the fairway:
   a pictorial autobiography.
      New York, Simon and Schuster, 1978. London, S. Paul,
      1980. Includes over 300 photographs.

— *and* WIND, Herbert Warren   The greatest game of all: my
   life in golf.
      New York, Simon and Schuster, 1969 and London,
      Hodder and Stoughton, 1969. 416pp.

OUIMET, Francis
OUIMET, Francis   A game of golf: a book of reminiscence.
      Boston, Houghton Mifflin, 1932. London, Hutchinson, 1933.
      254pp.

PALMER, Arnold
BISHER, Furman *and* OLDERMAN, Murray   The birth of a
   legend: Arnold Palmer's golden year, 1960.
      Englewood Cliffs, NJ, Prentice-Hall, 1972. 174pp.

GOLF DIGEST   Arnold Palmer.
      New York, Grosset and Dunlap, 1967. 159pp.

McCORMACK, Mark H.   Arnie: evolution of a legend.
      New York, Simon and Schuster, 1967. 250pp. British edition
      entitled Arnold Palmer: the man and the legend. London,
      Cassell, 1967. 318pp.

PALMER, Arnold   Portrait of a professional golfer.
      New York, Sterling Publishing, 1964. 110pp. London,
      Pelham, 1966. 110pp.

— *and* FURLONG, William Barry   Go for broke: my
   philosophy of winning golf.
      New York, Simon and Schuster, 1973. 252pp. London,
      Kimber, 1974.

PLAYER, Gary
PLAYER, Gary   Grand slam golf.
      London, Cassell, 1966. 133pp. London, Corgi, 1968. 190pp.
      (Paperback edition)

— *and* THATCHER, Floyd   Gary Player, world golfer.
Waco, Texas, Word Books, 1974. 193pp. London, Pelham,
1975. 157pp.

REES, Dai
REES, Dai   Golf today. London, Barker, 1962. 119pp.

— *and* BALLANTINE, John   Thirty years of championship
golf.
London, S. Paul, 1968. 180pp. Interesting autobiography by
former British Ryder Cup captain.

ROSS, Donald
GRANT, Donald   Donald Ross of Pinehurst and Royal Dornoch.
Golspie, Sutherland Press, 1973. 40pp.

RUTHERFORD, Ernest, 1st Baron of Nelson
MANN, Frederick George   Lord Rutherford and the golf
course.
Cambridge, The author, 1976. 33pp.

SANDERS, Doug
SANDERS, Doug *and* SHEEHAN, Larry   Come swing with me:
my life on and off the tour.
New York, Doubleday, 1974. 272pp. London, W.H. Allen,
1974. 222pp. British edition subtitled 'an autobiography'.

SARAZEN, Gene
SARAZEN, Gene *and* WIND, Herbert Warren   Thirty years of
championship golf: the life and times of Gene Sarazen.
Englewood Cliffs, NJ, Prentice-Hall, 1950. 276pp.

SHERIDAN, James
SHERIDAN, James   'Sheridan of Sunningdale': my 56 years as
a caddie-master.
London, *Country Life,* 1967. 144pp.

SMITH, Horton
SMITH, Horton *and* BENTON, Marion   The velvet touch.
Ann Arbor, Mich., Ann Arbor Press, 1965. 193pp.

SNEAD, Sam
SNEAD, Sam *and* STUMP, Al   The education of a golfer.
New York, Simon and Schuster, and London, Cassell, 1962.
248pp.

SPENCE, Johnny
SPENCE, Johnny *and* FRALEY, Oscar   Golf pro for God.
New York, Centaur House, 1965. 217pp. Paperback edition
entitled How to lose at golf. Wheaton, Il, Tyndale House,
1965. 192pp.

STRINGER, Mabel E.
STRINGER, Mabel E.   Golfing reminiscences.
London, Mills and Boon, 1924. 254pp.

TAIT, F.G.
LOW, John L.   F.G. Tait: a record, being his life, letters and
golfing diary.
London, James Nisbet, 1900. 304pp.

TAYLOR, John Henry
TAYLOR, John Henry   Golf my life's work.
London, Cape, 1943. 236pp.

THOMSON, Peter
THOMSON, Peter *and* ZWAR, Desmond   The wonderful world
of golf.
London, Pelham, 1969. 222pp.

TRAVERS, Jerome D.
TRAVERS, Jerome D. *and* CROWELL, James R.   The fifth
estate: thirty years of golf.
New York, A.A. Knopf, 1926. 259pp.

TREVINO, Lee
JACKSON, Robert B.   Supermex: the Lee Trevino story.
New York, Henry Z. Walck, 1973. 72pp. Book for younger
readers on the startling rise of Trevino from obscurity to one
of the best and most consistent players in the world.

VARDON, Harry
VARDON, Harry   The complete golfer.
   London, Methuen, 1905. 283pp. New York, McClure Phillips.
   Several later editions up to 1928, and reprinted in 1977.

— My golfing life.
   London, Hutchinson, 1933. 281pp.

VENTURI, Ken
VENTURI, Ken *and* FRALEY, Oscar   Comeback: the Ken
   Venturi story.
   New York, Duell, Sloan and Pearce, 1966. 192pp.

VON NIDA, Norman
VON NIDA, Norman *and* MACLAREN, Muir   Golf is my
   business.
   London, Muller, 1956. 210pp. London, Hamilton, 1957.
   191pp (Paperback edition)

WAY, Bucky
WAY, Bucky *and* PATTERSON, Jack   Sign 'em up, Bucky: the
   adventures of a sport agent.
   New York, Hawthorn Books, 1975. 229pp.

WETHERED, Joyce (Lady Heathcoat Amory)
WETHERED, Joyce   Golfing memories and methods.
   London, Hutchinson, 1933. 255pp.

ZAHARIAS, Mildred Didrikson
JOHNSON, W.O. *and* WILLIAMSON, N.P.   Whatta girl: the
   Babe Didrikson story.
   Boston, Little Brown, 1977. 224pp.

ZAHARIAS, Mildred Didrikson *and* PAXTON, Harry   This life
   I've led: my autobiography.
   New York, A.S. Barnes, and London, R. Hale,
   1956. 242pp. New York, Dell, 1975. (Paperback edition)

CHAPTER THREE

How To
Play The Game

Perhaps the majority — even the vast majority — of those who seek information about the game of golf do so in order to try to improve their game. This quest for knowledge has generated by far the largest segment of the golfing literature over the years. This literature is substantial, at least in terms of the total number of volumes or pages published. It is considerably less substantial in overall quality, although there are many significant landmarks against which the lesser authors can be measured. The title page of *The principles of golf* (1924) by J.M. Astle contains the observation that "the principles of golf are in themselves neither numerous nor abstract, but their application is difficult". If this statement is true — and many might agree with it — then it is even more remarkable that so many words and so many drawings, photographs and other visual aids have been produced over the years by so many people to explain such a few relatively simple fundamentals.

In trying to provide a systematic approach to the large number of works which fit into this section of the sourcebook it has been possible to identify many different approaches. A good deal of "cross classification" occurs since almost every permutation seems to have been explored. There are scientific treatises on the biomechanics of the golf swing through to works on the psychological aspects of the game. There are texts for beginners and for low handicap players, for the over-fifties and for boys, and on how to play with a wedge or a putter. There are books by leading professional players telling "how I do it my way" and there are volumes by pseudonymous amateurs who believe they have found the "holy grail" and want to pass it on to fellow sufferers who have yet to "break a hundred". There are books for left-handed players, and there are texts published in association with television pro-grammes and carrying reprinted articles selected from the pages of the golfing journals. And of course there are those items which advocate one particular technique balanced by those by some rival guru offering a completely opposite way forward.

In selecting items for inclusion and brief comment care has been taken to reflect all these aspects. What is not suggested is that any single approach provides the universal panacea to all golfing ills. The aim is rather to give information to allow the user of this volume to make a more informed selection to suit his own needs and purposes. In general, as elsewhere in this book, there is a concentration on more recent titles, though some earlier works of importance have been included. The standard of presentation of books published in recent years is often high, with imaginative use being made of visual material and colour presentations. As men-tioned elsewhere, many of the works in this chapter include more than just instructional material, and the seeker after information on, say, a well-known player or teacher might well find what they require from a perusal of a manual describing techniques that he or she advocates. In some volumes there is additional information on how to join a golf club, on the rules and etiquette of the game, on suitable dress, and on choice of clubs and other equipment. But basically all the items reviewed in this chapter have one overriding aim and that is to instruct.

H.B. Farnie's *Golfer's manual* (1857) has already been discussed in the context of historical works on the game but is the proto-type for most of the material that followed. Other books included in the historical chapter also contain a good deal of instructional material and have been mentioned in that context. The prolific Horace Hutchinson has made significant contributions to this sector. His *Hints on the game of golf* (1886), which appeared in many subsequent editions, was one of the earliest books devoted solely to acquiring technique. Hutchinson also edited *The new book of golf* (1912), which was also basically instructional. It had several distinguished contributing authors including Bernard Darwin and the pioneering lady golfer May Hezlet. One of the earliest works to be published in the United States was H.J. Whigham's *How to play golf* which appeared in 1897. For the more advanced player *The six handicap golfer's companion* (1909) by "Two of his kind" (a pseudonym for G.D. Fox) included chapters by two well-known golfing writers, H.S. Colt and Harold H. Hilton, who contributed a chapter on scientific wood play.

As photographic techniques improved a number of innovative texts started to appear. One of these was James Barnes's *A picture analysis of golf strokes* (1919) which included more than 300 photographs. It was particularly unusual in that these photographs were reversed for the benefit of the left-handed player. Pam Barton's *A stroke a hole* (1937) was also innovative in its time. By flicking through the pages of photographs the total golf swing in all its stages could be seen as in a motion picture. Innovation in golf teaching has produced several important landmarks, and these have stood the test of time. Some British coaches concentrated on the "hand action", and James Forrest was an advocate of this approach in his book *A natural golfer: hand action in games* (1938). Like some others before him, Forrest looks at the similarities with the game of cricket and of other sports such as hockey and tennis. Another British teacher, Eric Prain, produced a key document, in the opinion of many experts, with *Live hands* (1946). This was a slim volume of 55 pages which has been very influential. Percy Boomer's *On learning golf* (1942) is also regarded as a landmark in golf instructional books. Boomer developed a high reputation as a teacher and for his ability to communicate his expertise effectively. Another classic work is Ernest Jones's *Swing the clubhead and cut your golf score* (1952) which propagated the theory that the clubhead does the work. This book was reprinted by a New York publisher in 1977. A more recent work of importance, which takes the opposing view to Ernest Jones and his clubhead theory, is Merrins and Aultman's *Swing the handle not the clubhead* (1973). This book advocates concentration on the grip rather than worrying about what the clubhead is doing.

For many golfers, one of the best teachers of the game is the Scottish-American Tommy Armour, who was a considerable golfer who won several major championships but whose talents really flowered when he became involved in giving instruction. His books are all excellent basic works both for the beginner and for the golfer who wishes to check on his basic technique. *How to play your best golf all the time* (1954) has appeared in several editions and in paperback, and is regarded as one of the best manuals on golf technique yet published. Other books by Armour include *A round of golf with Tommy Armour* (1959) and *Tommy Armour's ABC of golf* (1967). Two other books with a high reputation are Mindy Blake's *The golf swing of the future* (1972) and *Golf: the technique barrier* (1978). These try to get away from the "do it my way" approach of the top players and return to some basic

PLAYER'S CIGARETTES

2 TOP OF SWING

C. S. Denny

3 FOLLOW-THROUGH

1 ADDRESS

BUNKER SHOT

Note club not grounded in the address. Right knee slightly bent, right shoulder lowered and pushed forward. Arms fairly straight.

problems involved in hitting a stationary ball.

The main problems for the human frame stem from the unnaturalness of such an activity, and this has been the subject of detailed analysis using modern scientific and sports medicine techniques. New technology in the form of computerised analyses of golf swings are the subject of Homer Kelley's *The golfing machine* (1971) and Michael Biddulph's *The golf shot* (1980), and the results of other investigations into this topic are given in David Williams's *The science of the golf swing* (1969) and Cochran and Stobbs's *The search for the perfect swing* (1968). The latter book reports the results of a comprehensive six-year study which was sponsored by the Golf Society of Great Britain and supervised by a distinguished panel of scientists from varying disciplines. Other scientific works of recent origin which include material on the biomechanics of the golf swing are James Hay's *The biomechanics of sports techniques* (second edition 1978) and Broer and Zernicke's *Efficiency of human movement* (1979) which has a relevant chapter.

Early books examining the swing itself include Burnham Hare's *The golfing swing simplified and its mechanism correctly explained*, which first appeared in 1913. There were several later editions of this slim work. Other works from the period included Daryn Hammond's *The golf swing* (1920) James Forrest's *The basis of the golf swing* (1925), and Peter Fowlie's *The technique of the golf swing* (1934). More recent works of some interest, which also attempt to teach the "long game", are Tommy Horton's *Golf: the long game* (1969), Flick and Aultman's *Square-to-square golf in pictures* (1974), which is subtitled in the British edition "An illustrated study of the modern swing techniques". David Lister's *I'd like to help the world to swing* (1977) is by a South African amateur player who believes, like many other enthusiastic amateurs (and many professionals for that matter), that he has discovered the elusive secret of how to swing a club to maximum advantage. A different approach is offered in *Joe Norwood's golf-o-metrics* (1978), which uses isometric exercises and relies on the build-up of leg and arm muscles in the player.

All golfers are aware of the old (and ungrammatical) adage "you drives for show, but you putts for dough", and it is the short game around the putting green where well over half of the total strokes are expended, especially among those with the higher handicaps. As specialisation becomes the norm it is no surprise to find plenty of material on this aspect of the game of golf. P.A. Vaile, who was a prolific producer of instructional manuals in the early years of the century, made an early contribution with *The short game* (1929). This was issued in Britain, with an introduction by Henry Longhurst, in 1936. Other books of substance include Tommy Horton's *Golf: the short game* (1969) — a companion volume to his work on the long game mentioned earlier — and some American publications by Phil Galvano, Gene Sarazen and others, and Paul Runyan. Galvano's *Secrets of accurate putting and chipping* appeared in 1957, Sarazen's *Your short game* in 1962, and Runyan's *The short way to lower scoring* was published by the magazine *Golf Digest* in 1980. Even more specific, in that they deal with the use of one particular club, are Doug Ford's *The wedge book* (1964) and the numerous volumes on the art of putting. An early book by former Open champion Willie Park on *The art of putting* appeared in 1920. This was followed by Jack White's *Putting* (1921) and P.A. Vaile's *Putting made easy* (1935). This last work was subtitled "The Mark G. Harris method" and was described by a later author (Paul Trevillion) as "the finest book on putting" — at least presumably until we get to Trevillion's own *Perfect putting method* of 1971 vintage. In between these there were books by Louis T. Stanley, Horton Smith and Bob Rosburg on what many regard as *the* most important facet of the game. Smith's *The secret of holing putts* (1961) is interesting because its author was widely regarded as one of the finest putters ever seen on a golf course. This book also contains a brief two-page bibliography on putting. Two other books are worthy of mention here. Tom Michael's *Golf's winning stroke: putting* (1967) is a lengthy and important text which was prepared with the assistance of the editors of *Golf Digest*. The same magazine also produced *All about putting* in 1973.

Golfing tactics are generally introduced in most instructional books, but Chinnock's *How to break 90 consistently* (1976) is somewhat unusual since it is mainly devoted to that aspect. An early work by British champion Ted Ray was also unusual in that it explained how to tackle inland golf courses at a time when most "real" golf in Britain was played on seaside links. The book was called *Inland golf*, and it was published in 1913.

Many instructional books are generated by the famous players. Most are, ostensibly, written by the great man (or woman), and largely sell on the strength of his or her name whether or not the knowledge imparted is useful and applicable to the average reader. Other books have been compiled by professional writers usually including brief contributions by leading players on one particular aspect of their game. George Beldam's *Great golfers: their methods at a glance* (1904) includes chapters by the leading players of his day. These were J.H. Taylor, James Braid, Harry Vardon, all professionals, and Harold H. Hilton, a leading amateur. This book also includes a brief chapter on the links between golf and cricket. Bernard Darwin's *Six golfing shots by six famous players* (1927) is a similar, but much slimmer, volume, and includes contributions from Abe Mitchell, George Duncan, J.H. Taylor, James M. Barnes, James Braid and Arnaud Massy. Much more recently Nicholas Tremayne's *Golf: how to become a champion* (1975) analyses the strengths and weaknesses of past champions, and is by no means a conventional type of instructional work. Another unusual approach was *Golf as I play it* (1940) by Richard D. Chapman and Ledyard Sands, which contained the results of 28 questionnaires sent to top players.

One of the first works by individual golfers was James Braid's *Advanced golf* (1908). It contains much on technique, and also includes information on the planning of golf courses and on golf equipment. Another famous British player, Harry Vardon, produced several books of instruction including *How to play golf* (1912), *Success at golf* (1912) and *Progressive golf* (1920). Henry Cotton's many books start with his *Golf* (1931). Most of his work belongs in this area, though some references are included in the historical and biographical literature.

Of the leading Americans, Bobby Jones contributed several important works including *Bobby Jones on golf* (1966). Ben Hogan also produced some notable books including *The modern fundamentals of golf* (1957), which was re-issued and reprinted many times. The material was prepared with the help of leading golfing writer Herbert Warren Wind and originally appeared in the American journal *Sports Illustrated*. Another important work by Hogan was *Power golf* (1948) which was updated and re-issued in paperback and other formats several times over the following 20 years. Hogan's contemporary, Sam Snead, also produced several interesting and useful manuals including *Sam Snead teaches you his simple key approach to golf* (1975) and the much earlier *Natural golf* (1953). Arnold Palmer's philosophies are outlined in various books published between 1961 and 1973. These include *Situation golf* (1970), which was published in Britain as *Arnold Palmer's golf tactics,* and *Four hundred and ninety five golf lessons* (1973). Other American master golfers

61

proferring advice include Lee Trevino in *I can help your game* (1971) and *Swing my way* (1978), and Tommy Bolt in *How to keep your temper on the golf course* (1969). Bolt was notorious in his earlier years for his uncontrollable outbursts but has mellowed over the years. His book avoids technical jargon and gives some useful hints on the psychological side of the game. Finally in this section it is appropriate to mention the output of Jack Nicklaus, whose awesome technique and amazing consistency at the highest level have meant that most golfers would regard any suggestions by him as worthy of attention. There is no lack of material for them to investigate, with many of the books mainly consisting of minimal text and many illustrations. Typical of the latter are the three volumes in the series *The best way to better golf* (1968-1971). Others, such as *Total golf techniques* (1977), originally appeared as articles in the magazine *Golf Digest*. Previous works, *Take a tip from me* (1968) and *My 55 ways to lower your golf score* (1964) date back to the earlier years of Nicklaus's professional career.

South African Gary Player has also published a series of instructional books, starting in 1962 with *Play golf with Player*. Leading British professionals Tony Jacklin and Peter Alliss have also made useful contributions. Alliss' *Easier golf*, written in collaboration with Paul Trevillion, was originally published in 1969 and was re-issued in 1977. Jacklin, apart from writing his own book, was also involved with broadcaster Michael Barratt in *Golf with Tony Jacklin* (1978) which is subtitled "Step by step a great professional shows an enthusiastic amateur how to play every stroke of the game".

Though many look to the leading names for advice, many of the best golf instructional books are the work of the top teaching professionals, and the name of John Jacobs is high on any list of experts in this area. Jacobs has produced several important texts, usually in collaboration with professional writers. These include *Golf* with John Stobbs (1963), *Practical golf* (1972) and *John Jacobs analyses golf's superstars* (1974), both with Ken Bowden, and *Golf doctor* (1979) with Dick Aultman. American Bob Toski is of similar stature as a teaching professional, and his books on golfing technique date back to *Beginner's guide to golf* (1955). Other titles which warrant attention include *The touch system for better golf* (1971) and *Bob Toski's complete guide to better golf* (1977). Toski's reputation is such that many of the leading players, both professional and amateur, turn to him for advice when their game needs attention. Two British teaching professionals who emphasise good hand action are Ken Adwick and Ken Redford. Adwick's books are highly regarded. They include *Golf* (1975) and *The X-ray way to master golf* (1970). Redford, with Nick Tremayne, produced *Success in golf* in 1977, and this too is an excellent manual. Another simple but excellent basic text is C.J. Naden's *Golf* (1970), as is Johnson and Johnstone's *Golf: a positive approach* (1975). This latter book also includes useful information on the selection of the right equipment. Jack Grout merits some attention if only because of his most famous pupil, and the title of his book explains all. This is *Let me teach you golf as I taught Jack Nicklaus* (1975), which appeared in Britain in 1977.

The advent of televised golf, and especially the use of the medium for instructional purposes, has also sparked off associated literature. *Play better golf with John Jacobs* (1969) was based on a Yorkshire Television series, and *Play golf with Peter Alliss* (1977) and *Master golf* (1978) by Neil Coles were also prepared for use with later series on different television channels. As has been suggested by the frequent mention of leading golf magazines, much instructional material starts out as articles within their pages. The American journals in particular produce some excellent texts in this way. Typical examples are *Golf Magazine's Winning pointers from the pros* (1965), in which the instructional editors are Gene Sarazen and Peggy Kirk Bell, and Fishman's *Short cuts to better golf* (1979) which is a carefully selected compendium of items from the previous 20 years of the same journal. This covers the basic fundamentals in a well-written and well-illustrated presentation. Before touching on books aimed at particular sections of the golfing fraternity brief comments on a final category of general instructional works are appropriate. These are written by unknown amateurs who believe they have discovered some basic truth and, because of their close identification with others like themselves who are striving to improve, feel that they can communicate their ideas effectively. One such was Robert Susswell, whose books appeared under the pseudonym of "Mr X". Susswell was a retired London businessman, and the material published appeared originally in the magazine *Golf Monthly*. The first was entitled *Golf Monthly's lessons with Mr. X* (1968), the second, *More lessons with Mr. X,* appeared in 1971, and the third, *Beginner's guide to golf,* was published in 1973. All are better than average instructional manuals.

Since golf is (or has generally been) a relatively expensive game to participate in, many of those playing the game are in the older and more affluent age groups. It is also a game which does not depend totally on a high level of physical fitness and can be played to a relatively advanced age. Nevertheless, physical fitness is important, and some authors have produced material to encourage it. Two books in this category are M.E. Deyo's *The easy way to stay in shape for golf* (1971), which outlines suitable physical exercises for the golfer, and Pratt and Jennison's *Year-round conditioning for part-time golfers* (1979), which also suggests a programme to improve the golfer's physical condition. The older golfer is well catered for in the literature, with a number of volumes aimed directly at his special needs. The first to be targetted directly at this group was G.M. Bottome's *Golf for the middle-aged and others* (1946). Others with similar titles and objectives include H.A. Hattstrom's *Golf after forty* (1946), Scott and Cousins' *Golf for the not-so-young* (1960), *Paul Runyan's book for senior golfers* (1963), Gene Sarazen's *Better golf after fifty* (1967), and Sam Snead's *Golf begins at forty* (1978). In the United States in particular many golfers who can afford to do so retire to the southern states or California, where golf is possible all the year round, and many golf resorts with special housing for older people have been developed. Robert O'Byrne's *Senior golf* (1977) covers much more than instruction, and deals with health care, retirement locations, and other information of relevance to the older player.

Although senior in age many older players are also beginners, and some of the instructional literature aims particularly at this market. Henry Hughes's *Golf for the late beginner* (1911) was an early work in this field, and many others with similar titles or aspirations have appeared over the years. One that is highly recommended by many experts is Reg Knight's *Golf for beginners* (1970), and others worth picking out of the pack are Mac Hunter's *Golf for beginners* (1973), Billye Ann Cheatum's *Golf* (Second edition 1975) and Alex Hay's *The golf manual* (1980). The last named includes sections on the rules of the game, etiquette, turning professional, and other matters.

Turning professional is not likely to affect the elderly beginner, but it may well be of interest to the junior. A sizeable literature has been generated for the younger player. Bobby Jones's *Group instruction in golf* (1939) is a handbook for schools and colleges, and a British work aimed at teachers is Hicks and Griffin's *Golf manual for teachers* (1949). In the United Kingdom the work of the Golf Foundation is central to golf encouragement of the young, and its activities and publications are described more fully in Chapter 7. One work which it strongly recommends is *Golf Digest's Better golf for boys* (1965), and its own brief work *Golf,* published in the National Westminster Bank sport coaching series, is also useful. Other valuable texts aimed at children and young people include Vivien Saunders' *The young golfer* (1977), Parker Smith's *Golf techniques* (1973), D.C.N. Hudson's *Your book of golf* (1967) and David Thomas' *Instructions to young golfers* (1959).

Women's golf also boasts its own instructional material dating back to *Our lady of the green* by Louie MacKern and M. Boys and published in 1899. James Braid's *The ladies field golf book* (1908) was another early work, and included some interesting advertisements for dress and equipment on its end papers in addition to having a chapter on the layout of ladies golf courses in the text. At that time ladies were not always welcome on "real" golf courses – a condition which exists to this day in some of the more conservative clubs. Some of the leading women players did, as their male colleagues had also done, write their own manuals. Cecil Leitch and Eleanor Helme produced several works between them in the earlier years of the twentieth century, and in the post-World War II period leading American players also produced some useful books. These included Patty Berg's *Golf for women illustrated* (1951), Louise Suggs's *Par golf for women* (1953) and *Golf for women* (1960) in which her co-authors represented some of the leading professionals and teachers of the period. In Britain, Enid Wilson in *Golf for women* (1964) and Jessie Valentine with *Better golf – definitely* (1967) also made useful contributions to the available literature. Even more recently three more excellent books have appeared. These are Sharron Moran's *Golf is a woman's game* (1971), which is a splendid book for the beginning woman golfer, Sandra Haynie's *Golf* (1975) and Vivien Saunders's *The complete woman golfer* (1975), which is particularly good in dealing with "trouble shots".

The left-handed golfer is not totally forgotten by the teachers of golf, and *The left-hander from New Zealand* (1965) is a book of instruction by one of the top players, Bob Charles. Another work aimed specifically at this market is Stewart and Gunn's *Left handers golf-book* (1976).

The interesting and significant literature which has developed around the mental approach to golf concludes this chapter. Of all games, golf is probably more "in the mind" than most, and this has long been recognised by those who attempt to play it. Haultain's *The mystery of golf* (1908) was probably the first book to deal specifically with this side of the game, and has become something of a classic of the literature. A new edition with a foreword by the foremost American golfing writer Herbert Warren Wind appeared in 1965. Other relatively early works in this rarefied sector, which abounds with qualified medical doctors and psychiatrists, are Schon's *The psychology of golf* (1922), Bailey's *The brain and golf* (1923) and Hyslop's *Mental handicaps in golf* (1927). Bailey's book is subtitled "Some hints for golfers from modern medical science" and is a fascinating work which tries to understand mental attitudes to the game. The book includes a more down-to-earth chapter on the game's theory and practice from Bernard Darwin. Hyslop's work is also noticeable, mainly perhaps because it is published by a well-known medical publishing house, Bailliere Tindall. In more recent times this aspect has been pursued just as diligently, and additional angles have been explored in such books as Heise's *Super golf with self hypnosis* (1962) and Michael Murphy's *Golf in the kingdom* (1973) which dabbles in the oriental philosophies to provide new approaches to the game. This is an unusual work and very difficult to classify in the golf literature. Other more conventional approaches to the psychology of the game include Nieporte and Sauers' *Mind over golf* (1968) which looks at how the top professionals handle what the authors call "the mysterious mental side of golf". Gary Wiren and an educational psychologist, Richard Coop, joined forces to produce *The new golf mind* (1978) which suggests that brain power is the key to improved performance, and British author Sandy Dunlop in his *Golfing bodymind* (1980) discusses the understanding of the relationship between the mind and the body and between the mental and emotional aspects of the game. Other recent American publications on the psychological aspects of golf include Charles Kemp's *Smart golf* (1974), David C. Morley's *Golf and the mind* (1976) and Orrin J. Hunt's *The joy of golf* (1977).

BIBLIOGRAPHY

A.Q., *pseud.*   The swing in golf and how to learn it.
London, A. and C. Black, 1919. 82pp. Several later editions.

ACREE, Edward, HUTCHISON, Jock *and* HUTCHISON, Bill
Golf simplified.
Chicago, Ziff-Davis, 1946. 118pp.

ADWICK, Ken   Golf, edited by James Green.
London, Pelham, 1975. 75pp. (Pelham pictorial sports)

— Ken Adwick's alphabet of golf, edited by James Green.
London, Pelham, 1973. 201pp.

— *and* GREEN, James   X-ray way to master golf.
London, Pelham, 1970. 167pp. Advocates the importance of
good hand action.

ALLISS, Percy   Better golf.
London, A. and C. Black, 1926. 152pp. Second edition 1933.

— Making golf easier.
Edinburgh, Stoddart and Malcolm, 1933. 51pp.

ALLISS, Peter *and* LAIDLAW, Renton   Play golf with Peter
Alliss, edited by Gordon Menzies.
London, British Broadcasting Corporation, 1977. 128pp.

67

— *and* TREVILLION, Paul   Easier golf.
London, S. Paul, 1969. New York, Barnes, 1972. Second
edition London, S. Paul, 1977. 142pp.

ANNARINO, A.   Golf: individualized instructional program.
Englewood Cliffs, NJ, Prentice-Hall, 1973.

ARMOUR, Tommy   How to play your best golf all the time.
Second edition London, Hodder and Stoughton, 1971,
159pp. Originally published in 1954, with a paperback
edition in 1965. Paperback edition (second edition)
Greenwich, Ct., Fawcett World, 1976.

— A round of golf with Tommy Armour.
New York, Simon and Schuster, 1959. 145pp. London,
Hodder and Stoughton, 1960. 145pp.

— Tommy Armour's ABC of golf.
New York, Simon and Schuster and London,
Hodder and Stoughton, 1967. 187pp.

ARNOLD, A.E.   Putting and spared shots.
London, Methuen, 1939. 74pp.

ASTLE, M.J.   The principles of golf.
Edinburgh, Chambers, 1924. 108pp. Second edition 1925.

AULTMAN, Dick *and* BOWDEN, Ken   The masters of golf:
learning from their methods.
London, S. Paul, 1976. 191pp. Published in the United States
as The methods of golf's masters: how they played and what
you can learn from them. New York, Coward, McCann and
Geoghegan, 1975. Bibliography on pages 189-191.

— *and* editors of GOLF DIGEST   Learn to play golf.
Chicago, Rand McNally, 1969. 72pp.

— The square-to-square golf swing: model method for the modern
player.
New York, Simon and Schuster, 1975. 127pp.

BAILEY, Charles William   The brain and golf: some hints for golfers from modern mental science.
London, Mills and Boon, 1923. 96pp. Second edition 1924. Boston, Small Maynard, 1924. Includes a chapter on theory and practice by Bernard Darwin.

— The professor on the golf links: some sidelights on golf from modern science.
London, Silar Birch, 1925. 91pp.

BAKER, Stephen   How to play golf in the low 120's.
Englewood Cliffs, NJ, Prentice-Hall, 1977. 92pp. Originally published in 1962.

BARBER, Jerry   The art of putting.
Los Angeles, The author, 1967. 24pp.

BARNES, James M.   A guide to good golf.
London, John Lane and New York, Dodd Mead, 1925. 137pp. Barnes won the 1925 Open Championship.

— A picture analysis of golf strokes: a complete book of instruction.
Philadelphia, Lippincott, 1919. 252pp.

BARRATT, Michael   Golf with Tony Jacklin: step by step a great professional shows an enthusiastic amateur how to play every stroke of the game.
London, A. Barker, 1978. 136pp.

BARTON, Pam   A stroke a hole.
London, Blackie, 1937. 88pp.

BASSLER, Charles and GIBSON, Nevin H.   You can play par golf.
New York, Barnes and Yoseloff, 1976. 102pp. Large type edition — very useful for the golfer with bad eyesight!

BEARD, Frank   Shaving strokes.
New York, Grosset and Dunlap, 1970. 126pp. Collection of tips which first appeared in syndicated newspaper columns.

BEGBIE, Harold   J.H. Taylor, or the inside of a week.
London, Mills and Boon, 1925. 107pp.

BELDAM, George W.   Golfing illustrated.
London, Gowans and Gray, 1980. 70pp. (Gowan's practical
picture books, no. 2).

— Great golfers: their methods at a glance.
London, Macmillan, 1904. 480pp. Includes contributions by
Harold H. Hilton, J.H. Taylor, James Braid, Alex Herd and
Harry Vardon.

— The world's champion golfers: their art disclosed by the ultra-
rapid camera.
London, Photocrom Co., 1924. Eleven books in the series.

— and TAYLOR, J.H.   Golf faults illustrated.
London, George Newnes, 1905. 175pp. Reprints of a series
of articles originally appearing in a sports magazine.

BELL, Peggy Kirk and CLAUSSEN, Jerry   A woman's way to
better golf.
New York, Dutton, 1966. 128pp. London, Cassell, 1967.
128pp.

BENSON, E.F. and MILES, E.H., eds.   A book of golf.
London, Hurst and Blackett, 1903. 308pp. Contributions by
James Braid, J.A.T. Braunston, Horace G. Hutchinson and
others.

BERG, Patty   Golf for women illustrated.
Second edition. London, Cassell, 1951. 72pp. Originally
published in the United States as Golf illustrated. New
York, Roland Press, 1950. 72pp.

— Inside golf for women.
Chicago, Contemporary Books, 1977. 86pp.

— and DYPWICK, Otis   Golf.
New York, Barnes, 1941. 81pp.

70

BERKELEY, Randal Thomas Mowbray Rawson, 8th Earl of
Sound golf: by applying principles to practice.
London, Seeley Service, 1936. 205pp. Part I Help for the
average golfer. Part II Advanced golf.

BERNARDONI, Gus   Golf God's way.
Coral Stream, Il., Creation House, 1978. 224pp.

BIDDULPH, Michael W.   The golf shot.
London, Heinemann, 1980. 116pp. Attempts to analyse
shotmaking by computerised and scientific methods. Bibliography of technical references page 113.

BLAKE, Mindy   Golf: the technique barrier.
London, Souvenir Press, 1978. 115pp.

— The golf swing of the future.
London, Souvenir Press, 1972. London, Corgi, 1974. 125pp.
(Paperback edition)

BOARD, John A.   The right way to become a golfer.
Kingswood, Elliot Right Way Books, 1948. 124pp. Second
edition 1952.

BOLT, Tommy and GRIFFITH, William C.   How to keep your
temper on the golf course.
New York, McKay, 1969. 145pp. London, Pelham, 1970.
145pp.

BOOMER, Percy   On learning golf.
London, John Lane, 1942. 215pp. Second edition, 1946.
New York, Knopf, 1946. 258pp.

BOROS, Julius   How to play golf with an effortless swing.
Englewood Cliffs, NJ, Prentice-Hall, 1964. 158pp.
Kingswood, World's Work, 1965. 158pp.

— How to play par golf.
New York, Prentice-Hall, 1953. 191pp. Kingswood, World's
Work, 1957. 191pp.

— Swing easy, hit hard.
New York/London, Harper and Row, 1965. 158pp.
New York, Cornerstone, 1968. (Paperback edition)

BOTTOME, George McDonald   Golf for the middle-aged and
others.
London, Faber, 1946. 66pp.

— and HERON, John   Modern golf.
London, Faber, 1949. 104pp.

BRAID, James   Advanced golf: or, hints and instruction for
progressive players.
London, Methuen, 1908. 322pp.

— The ladies field golf book.
London, George Newnes, 1908. 86pp.

BREWER, Gay   Gay Brewer shows you how to score better
than you swing.
South Norwalk, Ct., *Golf Digest* and London, S. Paul, 1968.
160pp.

BRINTON, Alan   Mr. and Mrs. Golfer cut their handicaps.
London, *News Chronicle,* 1955. 29pp.

BROER, Marion R. *and* ZERNICKE, Ronald F.   Efficiency of
human movement.
Philadelphia, Saunders, 1979. 427pp. Chapter 20 deals with
golf and especially the mechanics of the golf swing.

BROWN, George S.   First steps to golf.
London, Mills and Boon, 1913. 96pp. New York, James Pott.
Several later editions. Includes two chapters by Harold H.
Hilton.

BROWNING, Robert, H.K.   Golf with seven clubs.
London, Foyle, 1950. 93pp.

— Moments with golfing masters.
London, Methuen, 1932. 101pp.

BRUCE, Ben *and* DAVIES, Evelyn   Beginning golf.
Belmont, Ca, Wadsworth, 1962. 62pp. Second edition 1968.

BRZOZA, Walter C.   Putting secrets of the old masters: being
a selection of carefully selected, sometimes ancient notes,
pertaining to the perplexing part of the royal and ancient
game gathered mostly from old tomes writ by Willie Park, Jr.,
J. Travers, Walter Travis and others and done into a book.
Schenectady, NY, Parkway Classics, 1968. 25pp.

BURKE, Jack   The natural way to better golf.
New York, Hanover House, 1954. 151pp. London, Constable,
1955. 151pp.

— *and others*.   How to solve your golf problems.
South Norwalk, Ct, *Golf Digest,* 1963. 195pp. London,
Kaye, 1964. Co-authors are Byron Nelson, Johnny Revolta,
Paul Runyan and Horton Smith.

BURTON, Richard   Length with discretion.
London, Hutchinson, 1940. The author was British Open
Champion in 1939.

BUTLER, William Meredith   The golfer's manual.
London, Werner Laurie, 1907. 172pp. Philadelphia,
Lippincott. Covers all aspects of the game and has an
interesting chapter on course construction.

CAMERER, Dave   Golf with the masters: the secret to better
golf.
New York, Barnes, 1955. 159pp. London, Macmillan, 1955.

— , *ed.*   Improve your golf.
New York, Random House, 1958. 128pp. Contributors:
Jimmy Demaret, Mike Souchak, Cary Middlecoff, Sam Snead
and Louise Suggs.

CAMPBELL, Bailey   Golf lessons from Sam Snead.
New York, Duell, Sloan and Pearce, 1964. London, Muller,
1965. 126pp. New York, Hawthorn, 1973. (Paperback
edition)

CAMPBELL, Guy   Golf for beginners.
London, C. Arthur Pearson, 1922. 124pp. New York, F.A.
Stokes. Manual which includes chapters on appropriate dress
and "demeanour" and on golf course construction.

CANHAM, Peter   Introduction to golf.
Canberra, Australian Government Printer, 1975. 24pp.

CARR, Dick   You too can golf in the eighties: an effective
strategy for reducing strokes.
Hicksville, NY, Exposition Press, 1977.

CASPER, Billy   Golf shotmaking with Billy Casper.
South Norwalk, Ct, *Golf Digest* and London, Kay, 1966.
176pp.

— Good sense of golf.
Englewood Cliffs, NJ, Prentice-Hall, 1976.

— My million-dollar shots.
New York, Grosset and Dunlap and London, Cassell,
1970. 223pp.

— Two hundred and ninety five golf lessons, edited by Earl
Puckett.
Chicago, Follett, 1973. 80pp. Particularly good on the short
game.

CHAPMAN, Richard Davol *and* SANDS, Ledyard   Golf as I
play it: inside golf by 28 champions.
New York, Carlyle House, 1940. 158pp. Based on responses
to questionnaires sent to the players.

CHARLES, Bob *and* GANEM, Roger P.   Left-handed golf with
Bob Charles: a book of golf instruction.
Englewood Cliffs, NJ, Prentice-Hall, 1965. 127pp. British
edition published as The left-hander from New Zealand: a
book of golf instruction. London, Hodder and Stoughton,
1965. 139pp.

CHEATUM, Billye Ann   Golf.
  Philadelphia, Saunders, 1969. (Saunders physical activities
  series) Second edition 1975. 117pp. Bibliography on pages
  115-117.

CHERELLIA, George   All about hitting the sweet spot.
  Champaign, Il, Stipes Publishing Co., 1976.

— Tempo: the heart of the golf swing.
  Hollywood, Ca, Creative Sports Books, 1971. 68pp.

CHICAGO ATHLETIC INSTITUTE.   How to improve your golf.
  London, Kimpton, 1957. 72pp.

CHINNOCK, Frank   How to break 90 consistently.
  Philadelphia, Lippincott, 1976. 144pp.

CHUI, Edward F.   Golf.
  Pacific Palisades, Ca, Goodyear, 1969. 88pp. (Physical
  education series).

CLUBMATE, *pseud*. (Charles Kingsley Wilson)   Automatic
  golf.
  Northampton, The author, 1953. 24pp.

COCHRAN, Alastair *and* STOBBS, John   The search for the
  perfect swing: an account of the Golf Society of Great Britain
  scientific study.
  London, Heinemann, 1968. 242pp.

COLES, Neil   Master golf, edited by Alan Mouncer.
  London, Macdonald and Jane's, 1978. 64pp.

COMPSTON, Archie *and* LONGHURST, Henry   Go golfing.
  London, Duckworth, 1937. 105pp.

COTTON, Henry   Golf: being a short treatise for the use of
  young people who aspire to proficiency in the royal and
  ancient game.
  London, Eyre and Spottiswoode, 1931. 147pp. (The Aldin
  series)

— Hints on play with steel shafts.
Liverpool, British Steel Golf Shafts Ltd., 1933. 40pp.
Pamphlet issued after the ban on steel-shafted clubs was
lifted in 1929.

— My golfing album.
London, *Golf Life,* 1959. 248pp.

— My swing.
London, *Golf Life,* 1952. 144pp.

— The picture story of the golf game.
London, World Distributors, 1965. 158pp.

— Play better golf.
Newton Abbot, David and Charles, 1973. Previously
published as Henry Cotton says. London, *Country Life,*
1962.

— Study the golf game with Henry Cotton.
London, *Country Life,* 1964. 236pp.

— This game of golf.
London, *Country Life,* 1948 and New York, Scribners,
1948. 248pp.

COUSINS, Geoffrey   The handbook of golf: a guide to the
game and its techniques.
London, Pitman, 1969. 147pp. Includes chapters on the
history of the game, the evolution of clubs, rules and
etiquette, and has a glossary of terms.

COX, William James   Can I help you: the guide to better golf.
London, Benn, 1954. 95pp. Based on articles originally
appearing in *Golf Illustrated.*

— Improve your golf.
Harmondsworth, Penguin, 1963. 141pp.

— Play better golf.
London, Muller, 1952. 96pp.

76

— *and* TREMAYNE, Nicholas   Bill Cox's golfing companion.
London, Dent, 1969. 215pp. Aimed largely at the beginner
in golf.

COYNE, John, *ed.*   Better golf.
Chicago, Follett, 1972. 224pp. Collection of pieces by eleven
young golfers of 1971 including David Graham, John
Mahaffey and Tom Watson.

— The new golf for women.
New York, Doubleday, 1973. 223pp. Not for the beginner,
but a useful volume which tries to demonstrate that women
golfers can overcome any physical disadvantages.

CRANFORD, Peter G.   The winning touch in golf: a
psychological approach.
Englewood Cliffs, NJ, Prentice-Hall, 1961. 171pp. London,
Jenkins, 1962. 171pp.

CREMIN, Eric   Par golf, edited and arranged by John Fennell.
Sydney, Angus and Robertson, 1952. 127pp. One of the
relatively few golf books published in Australia.

DALY, Fred   Golf as I see it.
London, Sporting Handbooks, 1951. 126pp.

DANTE, Jim *and* DIEGEL, Leo   The nine bad shots of golf
and what to do about them.
New York, Whittlesey House,, 1947. 189pp. London,
Jenkins, 1948. 158pp. New York, Cornerstone, 1961.
(Paperback edition).

DANTE, Joe *and* ELLIOTT, Len   The four magic moves to
winning golf.
New York, McGraw-Hill, 1962. 218pp. London, Heinemann,
1963. 218pp. New York, Cornerstone, 1963. (Paperback
edition).

— Stop that slice.
New York, Crowell, 1953. 60pp. London, Jenkins, 1954.
112pp.

DARO, August F. *and* GRAFFIS, Herb   The inside swing:
key to better golf.
New York, Crowell, 1972. 124pp. London, R. Hale, 1973.
124pp.

DARWIN, Bernard   Hints on golf, with supplement on golfing
kit.
London, Burberrys, 1912. 55p.

— ,*ed.*   Six golfing shots by six famous players.
London, Dormeuil Freres, 1927. 46pp. Contributors include
Abe Mitchell, George Duncan, J.H. Taylor, James M. Barnes,
James Braid, and Arnaud Massy.

DAWKINS, George   Keys to the golf swing.
Englewood Cliffs, NJ, Prentice-Hall, 1976.

DEVLIN, Bruce   Play like the devil.
London, Angus and Robertson, 1967. 135pp. Tips from a
leading Australian touring professional.

DEYO, M.E.   The easy way to stay in shape for golf.
Davenport, Iowa, Information Services, 1971. 94pp.

DIAZ, Carroll   Golf: a beginner's guide.
Palo Alto, Ca, Mayfield Publishing, 1974.

DUNCAN, George   Golf for women.
London, Werner Laurie, 1907. 185pp.

— *and* DARWIN, Bernard   Present-day golf.
London, Hodder and Stoughton, 1921. 309pp. New York,
G.H. Doran, 1921.

DUNLOP, Sandy   The golfing bodymind.
London, Wildwood House, 1980.

DUNN, John   Golf from rabbit to tiger.
London, Thorsons, 1955. 134pp.

DUNN, John Duncan   Natural golf: a book of fundamental instruction which shows the golfer how to develop his own natural style.
New York, Putnams, 1931. 199pp.

DUNN, Seymour   Golf fundamentals: orthodoxy of style.
Lake Placid, NY, The author, 1922. 283pp. Reprinted New York, Arno Press, 1977. Important text which reduces the game to 20 basic techniques.

— Standardised golf instruction.
New York, The author, 1934. 153pp.

DYPWICK, Otis *and* JACOBS, Helen H.   Golf, swimming and tennis.
New York, Creative Education, 1962. For younger readers.

EAST, James Victor   Better golf in five minutes.
New York, Prentice-Hall 1956. London, Angus and Robertson, 1958. 202pp.

EDMONSTONE, C.G.   A study of golf from its mechanical aspect.
Erith, Kent, Edall Press, 1910. 68pp. Early "scientific" text on the golf swing.

ELLIS, Wes *and* SULLIVAN, George   All-weather golf.
Princeton, Van Nostrand, 1967. 108pp. Discusses adjustments to the game required in varying climatic conditions.

EVERARD, H.S.C.   Golf in theory and practice: some hints to beginners.
London, George Bell, 1896. 194pp. Several later editions.

FARRELL, Johnny   If I were in your golf shoes.
New York, Henry Holt, 1951. 87pp. British edition entitled The weekend golfer. London, Jenkins, 1952. 96pp.

FAULKNER, Max   Golf — right from the start.
London, Newnes, 1965. 120pp. (Beginner's guides)

— *and* SCOTT, Tom   Play championship golf all your life.
London, Pelham, 1972. 135pp.

— *and* STANLEY, Louis T.   The Faulkner method.
London, Hutchinson, 1952. 65pp.

FISHMAN, Lew *and* editors of GOLF MAGAZINE   Short cuts
to better golf.
New York, Harper and Row, 1979. 179pp.

FLICK, Jim *and* AULTMAN, Dick   Square-to-square golf in
pictures: an illustrated study of the golf swing.
Norwalk, Ct, *Golf Digest,* 1974. 125pp. British edition
entitled Square-to-square golf in pictures: an illustrated
study of the modern swing techniques. London, Collins,
1975. 128pp.

"FOLLOW THROUGH", *pseud.*   *(i.e.* James Sawyer-Shaw)
The essence of golf.
Oswestry, Hughes and Son, 1954. 70pp.

FORD, Doug   How I play inside golf.
Englewood Cliffs, NJ, Prentice-Hall, 1960. 146pp.
British edition entitled The brainy way to better golf.
London, S. Paul, 1961. 146pp.

— Getting started in golf.
New York, Cornerstone, 1964. Folkestone, Bailey Bros.
and Swinfen, 1970. 124pp.

— Start golf young.
Third revised edition. New York, Sterling, 1978. 144pp.
Earlier editions in 1955 and 1960 and published under the
title Golf.

— The wedge book.
South Norwalk, Ct, *Golf Digest* and London, Kaye, 1964.
126pp. (Kaye golf trilogy volume 2)

FORREST, James   The basis of the golf swing.
London, Thomas Murby, 1925. 60pp.

— Golf made easy.
London, Thomas Murby, 1930. 110pp.

— A natural golfer: hand action in games.
London, Thomas Murby, 1938. 97pp. New York, Dutton.

FOSTER, David   Thinking golf.
London, Pelham, 1979. 187pp. Called by one leading golf
writer "the most important work of research . . . since David
Williams produced 'The science of the golf swing' ".

FOWLIE, Peter   The science of golf: a study in movement.
London, Methuen, 1922. 128pp.

— The technique of the golf swing.
London, Methuen, 1934. 117pp.

FRALEY, Oscar   Golf in action.
New York, A.A. Wyn, 1952. 121pp.

FULFORD, Harry   Potted golf.
Glasgow, Dalcross, 1910. 148pp.

GALVANO, Phil   Secrets of accurate putting and chipping.
Englewood Cliffs, NJ, Prentice-Hall, 1957. 100pp.
British edition entitled The gentle arts of putting and
chipping. London, S. Paul, 1959. 100pp.

— Secrets of the perfect golf swing.
Englewood Cliffs, NJ, Prentice-Hall, 1961. London, S. Paul,
1962. 176pp.

GASKILL, Bud   Golf at a glance.
London, Arco, 1958. 128pp. New York, Arc Books, 1973.

GEIBURGER, Al and DENNIS, Larry   Tempo: golf's master
key, how to find it, how to keep it.
Norwalk, Ct, Golf Digest, 1980. 192pp.

GOLF DIGEST   All about putting.
New York, Coward, McCann and Geoghegan, 1973. 191pp.
London, Kaye and Ward, 1975. 191pp.

— Better golf for boys.
New York, Dodd Mead, 1965. 62pp. London, Kaye, 1966. 93pp.

— Eighty five-minute golf lessons from the world's greatest teaching professionals, compiled by the editors of *Golf Digest* magazine.
Englewood Cliffs, NJ, Prentice-Hall, 1968. 159pp. London, Pelham, 1969. 159pp.

— Golf: a golden pocket guide.
New York, Golden Press, 1968. 32pp.

— How to break ninety at golf.
Greenwich, Ct, Fawcett, 1967. 112pp.

— *and* TOSKI, Bob   Touch system for better golf.
New York, Simon and Schuster, 1971. 128pp.

GOLF FOUNDATION, *eds.*   Golf.
London, Training and Education Associates Ltd., 1974. 48pp. (National Westminster Bank sport coaching series)

GOLF MAGAZINE   Golf Magazine's handbook of putting.
New York, Harper and Row, 1973. 191pp. London, Pelham, 1975. 191pp.

— Tips from the teaching pros, by the editors of Golf Magazine.
New York/London, Harper and Row, 1969. 228pp.

— Winning pointers from the pros, instruction editors Gene Sarazen, Peggy Kirk Bell.
New York/London, Harper and Row, 1965. 274pp.

— Your long game.
London/New York, Harper and Row, 1964. 188pp.
Instruction editors: Jimmy Demaret, Gene Sarazen and Peggy Kirk Bell.

GOLF RESEARCH INSTITUTE   Guaranteed golf lessons: how to hit straight shots, how to hit long shots, why you hit bad shots.
New York, The institute, 1974. 63pp.

GRAFFIS, Herb   "Esquire's" world of golf: what every golfer
  must know.
  New York, *Esquire* in association with Trident Press, 1965.
  240pp. London, Muller, 1965. 269pp. Mainly instructional,
  but with sections on golf history, etiquette and other aspects.

GRAHAM, Lou *and* BIBB, John   Mastering golf.
  Chicago, Contemporary Books, 1978. 106pp.

GREENWOOD, George W.   Golf really explained, revised
  and brought up to date by Antony Briggs.
  London, Foulsham, 1961. 96pp. (New sports library)
  Earlier editions from 1926.

GROUT, Jack *and* AULTMAN, Dick   Let me teach you golf
  as I taught Jack Nicklaus.
  New York, Atheneum Press, 1975. 164pp. London, Cassell,
  1977. 164pp.

GUNN, Harry E.   How to play golf with your wife and survive.
  Matteson, Il, Greatlakes Living Press, 1976. 184pp.

HABER, James   Golf made easy: how to achieve a consistently
  effective golf swing.
  New York, Scribners, 1974. 154pp.

HAHN, Paul   Paul Hahn shows you how to play trouble shots.
  New York, McKay, 1965. 110pp. London, Pelham, 1966.
  110pp.

HALIBURTON, Tom   Rabbit into tiger.
  London, Heinemann, 1964. 168pp.

HAMMOND, Daryn   The golf swing: the Ernest Jones method.
  London, Chatto and Windus, 1920. 159pp.

HANDY, Ike S.   How to hit a golf ball straight.
  San Francisco, Cameron, 1967. 144pp. Written by an
  amateur who defies some of the accepted rules on the golf
  swing. Lucidly explained.

HARE, Burnham   The golfing swing simplified and its
    mechanism correctly explained.
    London, Methuen, 1913. 62pp. New York, Stokes. Several
    later editions up to 1920.

HATTSTROM, H.A.   Golf after forty.
    Los Angeles, Hall Publishing, 1946. 160pp. Kingswood,
    World's Work, 1951. 160pp.

HAULTAIN, T.A.   The mystery of golf: a brief account of
    games in generall; their origine; antiquitie; and rampance;
    and of the game ycleped golf in particular; its uniqueness, its
    curiousness and its difficultie; its anatomical, philosophical
    and moral properties; together with diverse concepts on other
    matters to it appertaining.
    Boston, Houghton Mifflin and London, Constable, 1908.
    151pp. Second edition revised and enlarged New York,
    Macmillan, 1910. 249pp. New edition New York, Serendipity
    Press, 1965, with a foreword by Herbert Warren Wind.

HAY, Alex   The golf manual.
    London, Faber, 1980. 192pp.

– The mechanics of golf.
    London, R. Hale, 1979. 136pp. New York, St. Martins Press,
    1979.

– Skills and tactics of golf.
    London, Marshall Cavendish 1980. 152pp.

– and ROBERTSON, Bill   The young golfer.
    London, Angus and Robertson, 1980. 96pp.

HAY, James G.   The biomechanics of sports techniques.
    Second edition Englewood Cliffs, NJ, Prentice-Hall, 1978.
    519pp. Chapter 11 deals with golf.

HAYNIE, Sandra   Golf: a natural course for women, edited by
    James Lynch and Carole Collins.
    New York, Atheneum Press, 1975. 208pp.

HEISE, Jack G.   How you can play better golf with self
  hypnosis.
      Hollywood, Ca, Wilshire, 1960. 128pp. British edition
      entitled: Super golf with self hypnosis. Kingswood, Elliott,
      1962. 109pp.

HELME, Eleanor E., *ed.*   The best of golf, by some best of
  golfers.
      London, Mills and Boon, 1925. 64pp.

— The lady golfer's tip book.
      London, Mills and Boon, 1923. 95pp.

HEROLD, Don   Love that golf: it *can* be better than you
  think.
      New York, Barnes, 1952. 137pp. Kingswood, World's Work,
      1953. 126pp.

HEXTER, Paul L.   You can play golf forever.
      Chicago, Contemporary Books, 1979. 65pp. Aimed at the
      over-fifties.

HICKS, Betty *and* GRIFFIN, Ellen J.   Golf manual for
  teachers.
      London, Kimpton, 1949. 312pp. Includes a bibliography.

HILTON, Harold H.   Modern golf.
      New York, Outing Publishing, 1913. 140pp.

HOGAN, Ben   Power golf, edited by Fred Honig.
      New and revised edition Greenwich, Ct, Fawcett, 1960.
      London, Muller, 1960. 144pp. First edition New York,
      Barnes, 1948. 166pp. London, Kaye, 1949. 190pp.

— *and* WIND, Herbert Warren   Five lessons: the
  modern fundamentals of golf.
      New York, Barnes, 1957. British edition entitled The modern
      fundamentals of golf. London, Kaye and Ward, 1957. 127pp.
      New York, Cornerstone, 1962. London, Transworld, 1965.
      (Paperback editions). Originally appeared as a series of
      articles in the American journal *Sports Illustrated*.

85

— and others   The complete guide to golf.
Indianapolis, Bobbs Merrill, 1955. 144pp. Co-authors are
Cary Middlecoff, Sam Snead, Tommy Armour and others,
and the book is a compendium of information from several
earlier titles.

HORTON, Tommy   Golf: the long game.
London, Batsford, 1969. 112p. (Batsford sports books)

— Golf: the short game.
London, Batsford, 1969. 111p. (Batsford sports books)

HOWARD, R. Endersby   Lessons from great golfers.
London, Methuen, 1924. 175pp.

HUDSON, D.C.N.   Your book of golf.
London, Faber, 1967. 54pp. For younger readers.

HUGGETT, Brian *and* WHITBOURN, John   Better golf.
London, S. Paul, 1964. 95pp.

HUGHES, Henry   Golf for the late beginner.
London, Thomas Murby, 1911. 93pp. New York,
McBride, Nast and Co., 1913. Several later editions. The
fifth edition 1922 was published by John Lane.

— Golf practice for players of limited leisure.
London, Thomas Murby, 1913. Second edition, with additional chapter 'How to reduce your handicap', 1922. 96pp.

HUNT, Orrin J.   The joy of golf.
Jacksonville, Fl, Convention Press, 1977. 145pp.
Psychological aspects of the game.

HUNTER, Mac   Golf for beginners.
New York, Grosset and Dunlap, 1973. 94pp.

HUTCHINSON, Horace G.   Hints on the game of golf.
Edinburgh, Blackwood, 1886. 75pp. Several later editions.

—, *ed.* The new book of golf.
London, Longmans Green, 1912. 361pp. Contributors are
May Hezlet, Bernard Darwin, James Sherlock, A.C.M.
Croome, and C.K. Hutchison.

HYSLOP, Theo B.   Mental handicaps in golf.
London, Bailliere Tindall, 1927. 111pp. Baltimore, Williams
and Wilkins Co.

IRWIN, Hale   Play better golf with Hale Irwin, edited by Keith
Mackie. London, Octopus Books, 1980. 152pp.

ITO, Chuzo, *ed.*   Golfer's treasures: being an alphabetical
arrangement of theories and hints from great golfers.
London, St. Catherine's Press, 1925. 311pp.

JACKLIN, Tony *and* REID, Iain   100 Jacklin golftips from
the Daily Express.
London, Beaverbrook Newspapers, 1972.

— *and* WOOD, Jack   Golf with Tony Jacklin.
London, Dent, 1969. 144pp. Published in the United
States as Golf step by step. New York, Bantam Books,
1970. 144pp. London, Pan Books, 1970. (Paperback edition)
1970.

JACOBS, John *and* AULTMAN, Dick   Golf doctor: diagnosis,
explanation and correction of golfing faults.
London, S. Paul, 1979. 126pp. Published in the United
States as Quick cures for weekend golfers.
New York, Simon and Schuster, 1979. 126pp.

— *and* BOWDEN, Ken   John Jacobs analyses golf's superstars.
London, S. Paul, 1974. 79pp.

— Play better golf with John Jacobs: based on the Yorkshire
Television series.
London, S. Paul 1969. 96pp. London, Arc Books, 1972.
Paperback edition.

— Practical golf.
New York, Quadrangle, 1972. 192pp. Paperback edition 1976.

— and STOBBS, John   Golf.
London, S. Paul, 1963. 160pp.

JESSOP, Joseph C.   Golf, revised by Mark Wilson.
Fourth edition. London, Teach Yourself Books, 1972. 224pp.
New York, McKay, 1975. Earlier editions in 1950, 1960 and 1968.

JOHNSON, Carole C. and JOHNSTONE, Ann Casey   Golf: a positive approach.
Reading, Ma, Addison Wesley, 1975. 172pp.

JONES, Ernest and BROWN, Innis   Swinging into golf.
New York, Whittlesey House, 1937. 150pp.
London, Nicholson and Watson, 1938. Second edition revised New York, McBride, 1946.

— and EISENBERG, David   Swing the clubhead and cut your golf score.
New York, Dodd Mead, 1952. 126pp. London, Jenkins, 1953. 116pp. Reprinted New York, Arno Press, 1977. 126pp.

JONES, Robert Tyre   Bobby Jones on the basic golf swing.
New York, Doubleday, 1969. 63pp.

— Bobby Jones on golf.
New York, Metropolitan Fiction Co., 1930. 112pp. Second edition 1931.

— Bobby Jones on golf.
New York, Doubleday, 1966, 246pp. London, Cassell, 1968. 246pp.

— Rights and wrongs of golf.
[no location] , A.G. Spalding, 1936. 53pp.

— and LOWE, Harold   Group instruction in golf: a handbook
   for schools and colleges.
      New York, American Sports Publishing Co., 1939. 63pp.
      (Spalding athletic library)

KELLEY, Homer   The golfing machine: the star system of golf.
   Seattle, Star System Press, 1971. 149pp.

KEMP, Charles F.   Smart golf: a study of the mental and
   emotional side of golf. Fort Worth, Branch-Smith, 1974.
   146pp.

KING, Leslie   The master-key to success at golf.
   London, Hodder and Stoughton, 1962. 157pp.

KNIGHT, Reg and SPICER, Sydney   Golf for beginners.
   London, Collins, 1970. 176pp. (Collins nutshell books)

— Learn golf backwards.
   London, Collins, 1965. 126pp.

LARDNER, George E.   Golf technique simplified: practical
   points for all players.
      London, Putnam, 1933. 240pp. United States edition
   entitled Cut your score: the book of commonsense golf.
   New York, Viking Press, 1933. 120pp.

LEITCH, Cecil   Golf.
   London, Thornton Butterworth, 1922. 254pp. Philadelphia,
   Lippincott.

— Golf for girls.
   London, Newnes, 1911. 91pp.

— Golf simplified.
   London, Thornton Butterworth, 1924. 126pp. Three
   manuals by one of the leading women golfers of the early
   part of the century.

LEMA, Tony *and* HARVEY, Bud   Champagne Tony's golf tips.
New York, McGraw-Hill, 1966. 147pp. British edition
entitled Tony Lema, champagne golf. London, Cassell,
1966. 106pp.

LISTER, David   I'd like to help the world to swing.
Scottsburgh, South Africa, Darville Investments, 1977.
150pp.

LOHREN, Carl *and* DENNIS, Larry   One move to better golf.
New York, Quadrangle, 1975. 123pp.

LONGHURST, Henry   Golf.
London, Dent, 1937. 335pp. (Modern sports series) Second
edition 1943. Third edition 1947.

— How to get started in golf.
London, Hodder and Stoughton,, 1967. 92pp. London,
Coronet, 1972. (Paperback edition) Aimed mainly at the
junior beginner.

LOWE, W.W.   Bedrock principles of golf.
London, Collins, 1937. 191pp.

McADAM, Cliff, *ed.*   How to break ninety/eighty/par.
New York, Winchester Press, 1973. 159pp. Directed towards
the better than average golfer who is playing to a low
handicap.

McALISTER, Evelyn   Golf for beginners.
Syracuse, NY, Ditton Books, n.d.

MacANDREW, J.   Golfing step by step.
Glasgow, Mitchell, 1910. 131pp.

McBAIN, J. *and* FERNIE, Willie   Golf.
London, Dean, 1897. (Dean's champion handbooks) Fernie
was professional at the Troon Golf Club and winner of the
Open in 1883.

MACBETH, James Currie   Golf from A to Z.
London, Putnam, 1935. 150pp.

McCALLISTER, George   Golfercises.
Studio City, Ca, The author, 1970.

McCARTHY, Coleman   Pleasures of the game: the theory free
guide to golf.
New York, Dial Press, 1977. 150pp.

McCORMICK, Bill   The complete beginners guide to golf.
New York, Doubleday, 1974. 130pp.

MACEY, Charles A.   Golf through rhythm.
East Grinstead, The author, 1957. 86pp. Author was
professional at the Crowborough Beacon Golf Club, Sussex,
England.

McGURN, Robert, WILLIAMS, S.A. and editors of GOLF
DIGEST.   Golf power in motion.
Englewood Cliffs, NJ, Prentice-Hall, 1967. 144pp. London,
Souvenir Press, 1968. 144pp. New York, Cornerstone, 1969.
(Paperback edition)

MACKERN, Louie and BOYS, M., eds.   Our lady of the green
(a book of ladies golf).
London, Lawrence and Bullen, 1899. 233pp.

McLACHLAN, Iaen   Billy Dunk's 'five under' golf: unique
introduction from Australia's brilliant World Cup golfer and
course record-breaker.
Sydney, Jack Pollard, 1972. 150pp. Second edition entitled
Attack the flag. Adelaide, Rigby, 1977.

— One hundred golf tips by leading Australian and New Zealand
golfers.
Adelaide, Rigby, 1973. 112pp. London, R. Hale.

— Swing to win: the story and techniques of leading proette Judy
Perkins.
Adelaide, Rigby, 1975. 95pp.

McLEAN, Jack   Why not beat bogey.
London, Blackie, 1937. 88pp. New York, M.S. Mill, 1938.

MANGRUM, Lloyd   Golf: a new approach.
New York, McGraw-Hill, 1949. 149pp. London, Kaye,
1949. 143pp.

MAPPIN, G.F.   The golfing you.
London, Skeffington, 1948. 128pp. Psychological aspects of
the game.

MARTIN, H.B.   Golf for beginners: easy lessons for the
novice, with valuable hints from the world's best known
authorities.
New York, Modern Sports Publishing, 1930. 98pp. Second
edition entitled Golf made easy 1932. Third edition entitled
How to play golf 1936.

— Pictorial golf: practical instruction for the beginner and valuable
hints for the star.
New York, Dodd Mead, 1928. 245pp. London, John Lane,
1929.

— What's wrong with your game.
New York, Dodd Mead and London, John Lane, 1930.
240pp.

MASON, Jack   Build yourself a golf swing by the seven steps of
the Mason method.
Southampton, The author, 1974. 32pp.

MASSY, Arnaud   Golf, translated from the French by A.R.
Allinson.
Third edition London, Methuen, 1922. 128pp. Originally
published (in French) Paris, Lafitte et Cie., 1911. First
English edition 1914. Second English edition 1922. Massy
was the first non-British golfer to win the Open Championship.

MAY, John Allan   Bedside duffer.
Boston, Christian Science Publishing, 1969. 64pp.

— Duffer's ABC.
Boston, Christian Science Publishing, 1970.

— Duffer's discoveries.
Boston, Christian Science Publishing, 1971.

— Duffer's guide, or golf for beginners in twenty lessons.
Boston, Christian Science Publishing, 1967.

— Duffer's progress.
Boston, Christian Science Publishing, 1968.

MAYER, Dick   How to think and swing like a golf champion.
New York, Crowell, 1958. 211pp. London, Macdonald,
1959. 191pp.

MERRINS, Eddie *and* AULTMAN, Dick   Swing the handle not
the clubhead.
Norwalk, Ct, *Golf Digest*, 1973. 128pp.

MICHAEL, Tom *and* editors of GOLF DIGEST   Golf's winning
stroke: putting.
New York, Coward, McCann, 1967. 189pp. London Souvenir
Press, 1968. 189pp. Important text on this facet of the game.

MIDDLECOFF, Cary   Advanced golf, edited by Tom Michael.
Englewood Cliffs, NJ, Prentice-Hall, 1957. 230pp. London,
Kaye, 1958. 230pp.

— Golf doctor.
New York, McGraw-Hill, 1950. 102pp. London, Kaye, 1952.
112pp.

— The golf swing, edited by Tom Michael.
Englewood Cliffs, NJ, Prentice-Hall, 1974. London, R. Hale,
1975. 230pp. Analyses the swings of some of the great
players from Harry Vardon to Arnold Palmer.

— Master guide to golf, edited by Tom Michael.
Englewood Cliffs, NJ, Prentice-Hall, 1960. 272pp. London,
Kaye, 1961. Above average book of instruction with
excellent illustrations.

MILLER, Johnny *and* SHANKLAND, Dale   Pure golf.
New York, Doubleday, 1976. 192pp. London, Hodder and
Stoughton, 1977. 192pp.

MR X *Pseud.* (*i.e.* Robert Susswell)   Beginner's guide to golf.
London, Pelham, 1973. 117pp. Englewood Cliffs, NJ,
Prentice-Hall, 1974.

— Golf Monthly's lessons with Mr. X.
London, Pelham, 1968. London, Sphere, 1968. (Paperback
edition)

— More golf lessons with Mr. X.
London, Pelham, 1971. 103pp.

MITCHELL, Abe   Down to scratch, edited and arranged by
J. Martin.
London, Methuen, 1933. Several later editions.

— Essentials of golf, edited and arranged by J. Martin.
London, Hodder and Stoughton, 1927. 191pp. New York,
George Doran.

— Length on the links: a book for players in all stages revealing
the secrets of the long ball, edited and arranged by J. Martin.
London, Methuen, 1935. 138pp.

MOONE, Theodore   Golf from a new angle: being letters from
a scratch golfer to his son at college.
London, Jenkins, 1934. 248pp.

MORAN, Sharron   Golf is a woman's game: or how to be a
swinger on the fairway.
New York, Hawthorn Books, 1971. 202pp.

MORGAN, John   Golf.
Wakefield, EP Publishing, 1976. 112pp. Boston, Charles
River Books, 1976.

MORLEY, David C.   The missing links: golf and the mind.
New York, Atheneum Press, 1976. 235pp. British edition
entitled Golf and the mind. London, Pelham, 1978. 235pp.

MORRISON, Alex J.   Better golf without practice.
New York, Simon and Schuster, 1940. 158pp.

— A new way to better golf, with introduction by Bernard
Darwin.
New York, Simon and Schuster, 1932. 187pp. London,
Heinemann, 1932. 179pp. Later editions in 1937 and 1946.

— A pocket guide to better golf.
New York, Simon and Schuster, 1934. 103pp.

MORRISON, Morie   Here's how in golf.
New York, Doubleday and London, Thorsons, 1950. 128pp.
1950. 128pp.

— Here's how to play money golf.
New York, Doubleday, 1953. 64pp.

MURPHY, Michael   Golf in the kingdom.
New York, Viking Press, 1972. 205pp. London, Latimer
New Dimensions, 1974. New York, Dell, 1973. London,
Abacus, 1976. 175pp. (Paperback editions)

MURRAY, Henry Arthur   The golf secret.
Sixth edition revised. Kingswood, Elliot Right Way Books,
1974. 126pp. Several earlier editions from 1952.

— More golf secrets: sequel to The golf secret.
Kingswood, Elliot Right Way Books, 1954. 140pp. New
York, Emerson, 1954. 160pp.

MYLES, Roderick W. and GORDIN Richard D.   Golf
fundamentals.
Indianapolis, Bobbs Merrill, 1973.

NADEN, C.J.   Golf.
New York, Franklin Watts, 1970. 64pp.

NAGLE, Kel *and others*   The secrets of Australian golfing
  success.
  Melbourne, Lansdowne Press, 1961. London, Kaye, 1961.
  127pp. Co-authors are Jim Ferrier, Peter Thomson and
  Norman von Nida.

NANCE, Virginia L. *and* DAVIS, Elwood C.   Golf.
  Third edition. William C. Brown, 1975. (Physical education
  activities series).

NEIL, Mark   The awful golfer's book.
  London, Wolfe, 1967. 56pp.

NELSON, Byron   Winning golf.
  New York, Barnes, 1946. 187pp. London, Macdonald, 1947.
  187pp.

— *and* DENNIS, Larry   Shape your swing the modern way.
  New York, Simon and Schuster, 1976. 127pp.

NICKLAUS, Jack   The best way to better golf.
  New York, Fawcett World, 1967. 128pp. London, Hodder
  Fawcett, 1968. 128pp.

— The best way to better golf. Number 2.
  New York, Fawcett World, 1968. London, Hodder Fawcett,
  1970. 127pp.

— The best way to better golf. Number 3.
  London, Coronet Books, 1971. 128pp. New York, Fawcett
  World, 1969. These three volumes are mainly illustrative
  material with minimal text.

— My fifty five ways to lower your golf score.
  New York, Simon and Schuster, 1964. 125pp. London, Hodder
  and Stoughton, 1965. 125pp.

— Playing lessons.
  London, Heinemann, 1980.

— Take a tip from me.
  New York, Simon and Schuster and London, Hodder and
  Stoughton, 1968. 125pp.

— Winning golf.
Columbus, Ohio, Grow Ahead Press, 1969.

— *and* BOWDEN, Ken   Golf my way.
New York, Simon and Schuster and Heinemann, 1974.
264pp. Paperback edition London, Pan Books, 1976.

— Jack Nicklaus lesson tee.
New York, Simon and Schuster, 1977. 157pp. British edition
entitled: Total golf techniques. London, Heinemann, 1977.
Originally published as a series of articles in the *Golf Digest*
magazine.

NIEPORTE, Tom *and* SAUERS, Don   Mind over golf: what
fifty pros can teach you about the mysterious mental side of
golf.
New York, Doubleday, 1968. 112pp. London, Cassell, 1969.
112pp.

NORWOOD, Joe, SMITH, Marilynn *and* BLICKER, Stanley
Joe Norwood's golf-o-metrics.
New York, Doubleday, 1978. 142pp.

NOVAK, Joe   Golf can be an easy game.
Englewood Cliffs, NJ, Prentice-Hall, 1962. 162pp. British
edition entitled Golf. London, Hennel Locke, 1964. 80pp.

— The Novak system of mastering golf.
New York, Doubleday, 1969. 54pp.

— Par golf in eight steps.
Englewood Cliffs, NJ, Prentice-Hall, 1950. 131pp. London,
Jenkins, 1951. 128pp.

OBITZ, Harry, FARLEY, Dick *and* TOLHURST, Desmond
Six days to better golf: the secret of learning the golf swing.
New York, Harper and Row, 1977. 180pp. London, Cassell,
1978. 180pp. Includes a useful chapter on 'Understanding the
flight of the ball'.

O'BYRNE, Robert   Senior golf.
New York, Winchester Press, 1977. 174pp.

OUIMET, Francis   Golf facts for young people.
New York, Century Co., 1921. 207pp.

PADGHAM, Alfred.   The par golf swing.
London, Routledge, 1936. 134pp.

PALMER, Arnold   The Arnold Palmer method.
New York, Dell, 1968. 235pp.

— Golf book: hit it hard.
New York, Ronald and London, Hodder and Stoughton,
1961. 142pp.

— My game and yours.
New York, Simon and Schuster, 1963. 158pp. London,
Hodder and Stoughton, 1965. Paperback edition London,
Corgi, 1969. 159pp.

— Situation golf.
New York, McCall, 1970. 83pp. British edition entitled:
Arnold Palmer's golf tactics. London, Kaye and Ward,
1970.

— and PUCKETT, Earl   Four hundred and ninety five golf
lessons.
Chicago, Follett, 1973. 128pp.

PARK, Willie   The art of putting.
Edinburgh, J. and J. Gray, 1920. 47pp.

PEPER, George F.   Scrambling golf: how to get out of trouble
and into the cup.
Englewood Cliffs, NJ, Prentice-Hall, 1977. 175pp.

PETNUCH, Andrew   Turn to golf.
Second edition New York, Carlton Press, 1975. 160pp.
First edition 1969.

PLATTE, Jules and GRAFFIS, Herb   Better golf through
better practice.
Englewood Cliffs, NJ, Prentice-Hall, 1958. 169pp. London,
Bailey and Swinfen, 1958.

PLAYER, Gary
— Gary Player's positive golf: understanding and applying the fundamentals of the game.
New York, McGraw-Hill, 1967. 119pp. London, Cassell, 1967. London, Corgi, 1970. 149pp. (Paperback edition)

— Golf secrets.
London, Pelham, 1964. 125pp. (Champions library).

— Play golf with Player.
London, Collins, 1962. 190pp. United States edition entitled Gary Player's golf secrets. Englewood Cliffs, NJ, Prentice-Hall.

— and HARRIS, Norman   Gary Player on fitness and success.
London, Sunday Times and World's Work, 1979. 102pp.

— and REID, Iain   Gary Player's golf class: 162 lessons for the weekender.
London, Beaverbrook Newspapers, 1975. 96pp. Several earlier editions with varying titles from 1967.

PLAYER, Gary and SULLIVAN, George   Gary Player's golf book for young people.
Norwalk, Ct, Golf Digest, 1980. 112pp.

PLUMRIDGE, Chris   How to play golf.
London, Hamlyn, 1979. 62pp.

PRAIN, Eric M.   Live hands: a key to better golf.
London, A. and C. Black, 1946. 55pp. Second edition 1947.

PRATT, William A. and JENNISON, Keith   Year-round conditioning for part-time golfers.
New York, Atheneum/SMI, 1979. 122pp. Suggests a programme to improve the golfer's physical condition.

PRICE, Charles   Golf, revised by Peter Ryde.
New edition London, A. and C. Black, 1976. 96pp. (Black's picture sports — a Sports Illustrated book). First edition published as Sports Illustrated Golf. Philadelphia, Lippincott, 1970. 73pp.

—, *ed.*   Pro pointers and stroke savers.
New York, Harper Bros., 1960. 253pp. London, H.
Hamilton, 1960. Instructional editors are Gene Sarazen,
Jimmy Demaret and Louise Suggs.

PROFESSIONAL GOLFERS ASSOCIATION   Golf.
11th edition. Wakefield, EP Publishing, 1975. 42pp.
(Know the game series)

RANKIN, Judy *and* ARONSTEIN, Michael   A natural way to
golf power.
New York, Harper and Row, 1976. London, Angus and
Robertson, 1976. 126pp. New York, Cornerstone, 1977.
(Paperback edition)

RAVIELLI, Anthony   What is golf?
New York, Atheneum Press, 1976.

RAY, Edward   Driving, approaching and putting.
London, Methuen, 1922. 47pp. New York, McBride.

— Golf clubs and how to use them.
London, Methuen, 1922. 55pp. New York, McBride, 1922.

— Inland golf.
London, Werner Laurie, 1913. 234pp. New York, James
Pott. Ray was Open Champion in 1912.

REDFORD, Ken *and* TREMAYNE, Nicholas   Success in golf.
London, John Murray, 1977. 86pp. (Success sportsbooks)

REES, Dai   Dai Rees on golf.
London, Duckworth, 1959. 176pp.

— Golf my way.
London, Heinemann, 1951. 88pp.

— The key to golf.
London, Duckworth, 1961. 127pp.

RHODES, Louis   Stop action golf: the driver.
Maplewood, NJ, Hammond, 1971.

ROBINSON, Larry   Golf secrets of the pros.
Greenwich, Ct, Fawcett and London, Muller,
1956. 144pp.

– New golf secrets of the pros, edited by Fred Honig.
Greenwich, Ct, Fawcett, 1959. 144pp. London, Muller,
1959.

RODRIGUEZ, Juan (Chi Chi)   Chi Chi's secrets of positive
golf.
New York, Viking Press, 1967. 78pp. London, Pelham,
1968. 74pp.

– and FITT, Chuck   Everybody's golf book.
New York, Viking Press, 1975. 152pp.

– and STROIMAN, Harry   Chi Chi's golf secret.
Des Moines, Iowa, The author, 1962. 32pp.

ROSBURG, Bob   The putter book.
South Norwalk, Ct, *Golf Digest* and London, Kaye, 1964.
125pp. (Kaye golf trilogy volume 3)

RUNYAN, Paul   Golf is a game.
New York, Calvert Distilling Corporation, 1939. 24pp.

– Paul Runyan's book for senior golfers.
New York, Dodd Mead, 1963. 149pp.

– and AULTMAN, Dick   The short way to lower scoring.
South Norwalk, Ct, *Golf Digest*, 1980. 175pp.

SANDERS, Doug   Compact golf.
New York, Crowell, 1964. 176pp. London, Kaye and Ward,
1967. 176pp.

SARAZEN, Gene   Gene Sarazen's commonsense golf tips.
Chicago, Wilson, 1924. 104pp.

– , DEMARET, Jimmy *and* BELL, Peggy Kirk, *eds.*   Your
long game.
New York, Harper and Row, 1964. 188pp.

— *and* GANEM, Roger   Better golf after fifty.
New York/London, Harper and Row, 1967. 121pp.

— *and* SUGGS, Louise, *eds.*   Your short game.
New York, Harper and Row, 1962. 203pp.

— *and others.*   The golf clinic.
Chicago, Ziff-Davis, 1949. 157pp. London, Kaye, 1950.
164pp. Co-authors are Sam Snead, Lloyd Mangrum, Jim
Ferrier, Ellsworth Vines and Ed Oliver.

SAUNDERS, Vivien   The complete woman golfer.
London, S. Paul, 1975. 144pp.

— *and* CLARK, Clive   The young golfer.
London, S. Paul, 1977. 112pp.

SCHARFF, Robert   Collier's quick and easy guide to golf.
New York, Collier, 1963. 96pp. New York, Collier
Macmillan, 1968. (Paperback edition)

— *and* editors of GOLF MAGAZINE   Handbook of golf
strategy.
New York, Harper and Row, 1971. 232pp. London, Cassell,
1973.

SCHMITT, Chuck   My golf clinic.
Venice, Fl, Sunshine Press, 1967. 31pp.

SCHON, Leslie   The psychology of golf.
London, Methuen, 1922. 120pp.

SCOTT, Tom   Club golfer's handbook.
London, A. Barker, 1972. 162pp. A particularly good book
for beginners with much on the rules, etiquette, joining a
club etc.

— Golf: begin the right way.
Newton Abbot, David and Charles, 1974. 127pp.

— , *ed.*   Golf with the experts.
London, Heinemann, 1959. 180pp.

— Golfing technique in pictures.
London, Hulton Press, 1957. Includes a chapter on golf history by A.J. Stott. Other contributions by leading British professionals.

— More golf with the experts.
London, Heinemann, 1965. 184pp. United States edition entitled Secrets of the golfing greats. New York, Barnes. Tips on different aspects of the game from 24 leading players

— *and* COUSINS, Geoffrey   Golf for the not-so-young.
London, P. Davies, 1960. 208pp. United States edition entitled Golf begins at forty-five. New York, Barnes.

SEYMOUR, Bert   All about golf: how to improve your game.
London, Ward Lock, 1924. 304pp.

SHANKLAND, Craig *and others*   Stroke-saving for the handicap golfer, edited by Peter Alliss.
London, Foulsham, 1979. 215pp. (Sports Illustrated book). Co-authors are Dale Shankland, Dom Lupo and Roy Benjamin.

SHAPIRO, Harold   Get golf straight.
Bristol, Abson Books, 1972.

SMARTT, Patrick   If you must play golf.
London, S. Paul, 1963. 127pp. Partly instructional and partly on golf club membership.

SMITH, Don   The young sportsman's guide to golf.
Edinburgh, Nelson, 1961. 95pp. (Young sportsman's library)

SMITH, Garden G.   Golf: with a contribution by Mrs Mackern.
London, Lawrence and Bullen, 1897. 104pp.

SMITH, Horton *and* TAYLOR, Dawson   The secret of holing putts.
New York, Barnes, 1961. London, Yoseloff, 1961. 156pp. Second edition entitled The secret of perfect putting. Los Angeles, Wilshire, 1963. Bibliography.

SMITH, J.S.K. *and* WEASTALL, B.S.   The foundations of golf: dedicated to the late beginner.
London, Methuen, 1925. 82pp. New York, McBride, 1926.

SMITH, Parker   Golf techniques: how to improve your game.
New York, Watts, 1973. 63pp. (Concise guide series) For younger players.

SNEAD, Sam   The driver book.
South Norwalk, Ct, *Golf Digest*, 1964. 126pp. (Kaye golf trilogy volume 1). Published in paperback entitled The driver. New York, Cornerstone, 1965.

— How to hit a golf ball from any sort of lie, edited by Mark Cox.
Garden City, NY, Garden City Books and Kingswood, World's Work, 1950. 74pp.

— How to play golf and professional tips on improving your score: also rules of the game of golf.
Garden City, NY, Garden City Publishing, 1946. 173pp.

— Natural golf.
New York, Barnes, 1953. 208pp. London, Burke, 1954. 192pp.

— Sam Snead on golf.
Englewood Cliffs, NJ, Prentice-Hall, 1962. London, Kaye, 1962. 146pp.

— Sam Snead's quick way to better golf.
New York, Sun Dial Press, 1938. 80pp.

— *and* AULTMANN, Dick   Golf begins at forty.
New York, Dial Press, 1978, 175pp. London, Hodder and Stoughton, 1979. 175pp.

— *and* SHEEHAN, Larry   Sam Snead teaches you his simple key approach to golf.
New York, Atheneum Press, 1975. British edition entitled Sam Snead's book of golf: keys to lifelong success. London, S. Paul, 1975. 178pp.

SPALDING, Anthony   Golf for beginners.
London, Link House, 1935. 56pp.

SPORTS ILLUSTRATED   Golf lessons from great pros: 113
golf lessons by 82 leading professionals.
Englewood Cliffs, NJ, Prentice-Hall, 1961. British edition
entitled Golf lessons from the pros. London, *Country Life*,
1962. 235pp.

— Golf tips from the top professionals, edited by Herbert Warren
Wind.
Greenwich, Ct, Fawcett, 1958. 144pp. London, Muller,
1958. Abridged from Tips from the top books 1 and 2 (*q.v.*)

— Tips from the top: 52 golf lessons from 27 leading professionals,
compiled by Herbert Warren Wind.
New York, Prentice-Hall, 1977. London, *Country Life*, 1956.
105pp

— Tips from the top. Book 2: 52 more golf lessons by 40 leading
professionals, compiled by Herbert Warren Wind.
New York, Prentice-Hall, 1956. London, *Country Life*,
1957. 105pp.

"STANCLIFFE", *pseud.* (*i.e.* Stanley Clifford)   The autobiography of a caddy-bag.
London, Methuen, 1924. 86pp.

— Golf do's and don'ts: being a very little about a good deal.
London, Methuen, 1902. 64pp. Several later editions.

— Quick cuts to good golf.
London, Methuen, 1920. 61pp. New York, Stokes, 1923.

STANLEY, Louis T.   Fontana golf book.
London, Collins, 1960. 128pp. Second edition 1960.

— Golf with your hands.
London, Collins, 1966. 256pp.

— Master golfers in action.
London, Macdonald, 1950. 143pp.

— Style analysis.
London, Naldrett Press, 1951. 104pp.

— Swing to better golf.
London, Collins, 1957. 256pp. New York, Crowell.

— This is golf.
London, W.H. Allen, 1954. 192pp. New York, Barnes.

— This is putting.
London, W.H. Allen, 1955. 192pp.

— The woman golfer.
London, Macdonald, 1952. 128pp. United States edition
entitled How to be a better woman golfer. New York,
Crowell.

STARK, A.   Physical training for golfers: improve your game
by "jerks".
St. Andrews, W.C. Henderson, 1937. 62pp.

STEWART, Earl and GUNN, Harry E.   Golf begins at forty.
Matteson, Il, Greatlakes Living Press, 1977. 163pp.

— Left handers golf book.
Matteson, Il, Greatlakes Living Press, 1976. 166pp.

STOBBS, John   Tackle golf this way.
London, S. Paul, 1961. 128pp. United States edition entitled
Anatomy of golf: technique and tactic. New York, Emerson,
1962. Revised edition entitled 'Tackle golf' London, S. Paul,
1975. 128pp.

SUGGS, Louise   Par golf for women.
New York, Prentice-Hall, 1953. 128pp. London, Harrap,
1954. 128pp.

— and others   Golf for women.
New York, Doubleday, 1960. 191pp. London, Muller, 1961.
191pp. Second edition New York, Cornerstone, 1963.
Co-authors are Marlene Bauer Hagge, Beverley Hanson,
Jackie Pung, Barbara Romack, Joyce Ziske and Ruth Jessen.

SWARBRICK, Brian   Every duffer's guide to good golf.
London, Pelham, 1973. 167pp. United States edition entitled
The duffers guide to bogey golf. Englewood Cliffs, NJ,
Prentice-Hall, 1973. 167pp.

TAYLOR, Joshua   The art of golf: with a chapter on the
evolution of the bunker by J.H. Taylor, ex-champion.
London, Werner Laurie, 1913. 161pp. New York, Outing
Publishing Co.

THOMAS, David   Instructions to young golfers.
London, Museum Press, 1959. 126pp.

– and WRIGHT, Ben   Modern golf.
London, Duckworth, 1967. 102pp. Excellent manual for the
average player.

THOMPSON, Kenneth R.   The mental side of golf: a study of
the game as practised by champions.
New York, Funk and Wagnalls, 1939. 153pp. London,
Muller, 1955. 157pp.

THOMSON, Ben   How to play golf.
New York, Prentice-Hall, 1939. 65pp. London, Pitman.
Several later editions.

TOLLEY, Cyril J.H.   The modern golfer.
London, Collins, 1924. 292pp. New York, A. Knopf.

TOSKI, Bob   Beginner's guide to golf.
New York, Grosset and Dunlap, 1955. 80pp.

– Play like the pros.
New York, Atheneum Press, 1975.

– The pros guide to better golf, edited by Dick Aultman.
New York, Grosset and Dunlap, 1975. British edition entitled
Bob Toski's guide to better golf. London, R. Hale, 1975.
48pp.

— The touch system for better golf.
Paperback edition New York, Bantam Books, 1979. (Original edition listed under Golf Digest q.v.)

— Twelve shortcuts to better golf, edited by Dick Aultman.
New York, Atheneum Press, 1974. 48pp. London, R. Hale, 1975. 48pp.

— *and* AULTMAN, Dick   Bob Toski's complete guide to better golf.
New York, Atheneum Press, 1977. 135pp.

— *and* FLICK, Jim   How to become a complete golfer.
Norwalk, Ct, *Golf Digest*, 1979, 288pp.

TOWNSEND, Peter *and* REID, Iain   Golf: one hundred ways to improve your game.
London, Barrie and Jenkins, 1977. 90pp.

TREMAYNE, Nicholas   Golf: how to become a champion.
London, Luscombe, 1975. 126pp. United States edition entitled Golf: how to become a champ. New York, Transatlantic, 1976.

TREVILLION, Paul   How to improve your golf.
New York, Collier Macmillan, 1974.

— The perfect putting method.
London, Pelham, 1971. 128pp. Trevillion "invented" a new putting style which had some popularity in the early 1970s.

— Save strokes like the stars.
London, S. Paul, 1970. 236pp.

— Tony Jacklin in play.
London, A. Barker, 1970. 121pp.

TREVINO, Lee *and* AULTMAN, Dick   Groove your golf swing my way.
New York, Atheneum Press, 1976. 184pp. British edition entitled Swing my way. London, Angus and Robertson, 1978. 184pp.

— *and* FRALEY, Oscar   I can help your game.
Greenwich, Ct, Fawcett, 1971. 155pp. London, W.H. Allen,
1972. London, Corgi, 1973. 160pp. (Paperback edition)

TURNESA, Jim   Twelve lessons to better golf.
New York, Prentice-Hall, 1953. 180pp. British edition
entitled Low score golf. London, Jenkins, 1953. 133pp.

TUTHILL, Max   Golf without gall.
London, Hutchinson, 1938. 102pp.

"TWO OF HIS KIND", *pseud. (i.e.* G.D. Fox)   The six handicap
golfer's companion, with chapters by H.S. Colt on golf generally
and Harold H. Hilton on scientific wood play.
London, Mills and Boon, 1909. 120pp.

VAILE, P.A.   Golf on the green.
New York, John Wanamaker, 1915. 108pp.

— How to learn golf.
New York, American Sports Publishing Co., 1922. 60pp.

— Modern golf. 1909.
London, A. and C. Black, 1909. 256pp. Second edition
1914.

— The new golf.
New York, E.P. Dutton, 1916. 289pp.

— Putting made easy: the Mark G. Harris method.
Chicago, Reilly and Lee, 1935. 95pp.

— The short game.
Chicago, Beckley-Ralston, 1929. 40pp. London, Duckworth,
1936. 136pp. The English edition has an introduction by
Henry Longhurst.

— The soul of golf.
London, Macmillan, 1912. 356pp.

VALENTINE, Jessie *and* HOUGHTON, George   Better golf — definitely!
   London, Pelham, 1967. 102pp.

VARDON, Harry   How to play golf.
   London, Methuen, 1912. 298pp. Philadelphia, D.W. Jacobs.
   Several later editions.

— Progressive golf.
   London, Hutchinson, 1920. 160pp. Several later editions.

— *and others*   Success at golf: hints for the player of moderate ability.
   London *Fry's Magazine*, 1912. 143pp. Boston, Little
   Brown, 1914. 116pp. The American edition has a chapter by
   Francis Ouimet replacing those by Jack White and Tom Ball.

"A VETERAN", *pseud.*   The secret of golf for occasional players.
   London, Methuen, 1922. 47pp. New York, McBride. Slim
   little volume explaining the use of the baffy, the cleek and the
   niblick among other things.

VON NIDA, Norman   Golf isn't hard.
   London, Sampson, Low, 1949. 91pp.

VROOM, Jerry   So you want to be a golfer?
   San Jose, Ca, The author, 1973. 48pp.

WEBBER, Louis *and* KENNEDY, Dennis   Golf manners.
   Universal City, Texas, The authors, 1968. 67pp.

WEETMAN, Harry   The way to golf.
   London, Ward Lock, 1953. 160pp.

— *and* BALLANTINE, John   Add to your golf power.
   London, Heinemann, 1963. 158pp.

WEISKOPF, Tom   Go for the flag: the fundamentals of golf.
   New York, Meredith Press, 1969. 88pp.

WEISS, Mike   100 handy hints on how to break 100.
New York, Prentice-Hall, 1951. 118pp.

WETHERED, Roger *and* WETHERED, Joyce   Golf from two
sides.
London, Longmans Green, 1922. 197pp. Second edition
1925. Mostly a "how to do it" book by two leading players
of the 1920s.

WHIGHAM, H.J.   How to play golf.
Chicago, Stone, 1897. 313pp.

WHITCOMBE, Charles A.   Charles Whitcombe on golf.
London, Alexander Ousley, 1931. 66pp.

— Golf.
London, Pitman, 1949. 150pp. Includes a section by Robert
H.K. Browning on the golf rules.

WHITCOMBE, Reginald A.   Golf's no mystery: a book for
golfers and beginners.
London, Dent, 1938. 127pp.

WHITE, Jack   Easier golf.
London, Methuen, 1924. 115pp. + photographs.

— Putting.
London, *Country Life*/Newnes, 1921. 48pp. New York,
Scribners.

WHITE, Ronald James   Golf as I play it.
London, G. Bell, 1953. 160pp. White was a leading British
amateur player.

WHITLATCH, Marshall   Golf for beginners and others.
New York, Outing Publishing, 1910. 280pp.
London, Fisher Unwin, 1910. Second and third editions
published in the United States by Macmillan in 1921 and
1923.

WILL, George   Golf the modern way.
London, *Country Life*, 1968. 176pp.

WILLIAMS, David   The science of the golf swing.
London, Pelham, 1969. 131pp. Important scientific analysis.

WILLIAMS, Evan *and* SHEEHAN, Larry   You can hit the golf
ball further.
Norwalk, Ct, *Golf Digest*, 1979. 127pp.

WILSON, Enid   Golf for women.
London, A. Barker, 1964. 84pp.

— *and* LEWIS, Robert Allen   So that's what I do.
London, Methuen, 1935. 127pp.

WILSON, Kenneth   It's all in the swing: self help for the
average golfer.
London, Putnam, 1947. 155pp.

— To better golf in two strides.
London, Putnam, 1938. 156pp.

WIREN, Gary   Golf.
Englewood Cliffs, NJ, Prentice-Hall, 1971. 118pp. (Sports
series). Wiren is one of the leading American teaching professionals and a former Director of Education for the Professional Golfers Association of America.

—,COOP, Richard *and* SHEEHAN, Larry   The new golf mind.
New York, Simon and Schuster, 1978. 160pp.

WRIGHT, Mickey   Play golf the Wright way, edited by Joan
Flynn.
New York, Doubleday and London, Cassell, 1962.
96pp.

YOGI, Count Hilary   Five simple steps to perfect golf.
Los Angeles, Nash, 1973. 138pp.

ZAHARIAS, Mildred "Babe" Didrikson   Championship golf.
New York, Barnes, 1948. 125pp. London, Sampson Low,
1949. 125pp.

CHAPTER FOUR

ESSAYS, FICTION AND HUMOUR

Much golf writing appears in the form of brief essays, many of which start out as contributions to newspapers and journals. Some of the more significant pieces are preserved by their inclusion in books of essays, bedside books and anthologies. This area of the literature includes some of the most accomplished writing on the game, and some of the greatest of the golfing writers have contributed to it. As with previous chapters, it has to be pointed out that some overlap is inevitable with other sections of this work as many such short pieces are primarily of historical, biographical or even instructional value. Others are items on the golf business in all its aspects, and on places to play the game both in the United Kingdom and abroad.

This chapter is also devoted to the fictional golfing material. Like another popular pastime, fishing, the game of golf is particularly prone to exaggerated accounts of prowess and success which may not be entirely untrue but undoubtedly gain much in the telling and re-telling of the tale. There are golfers who much prefer the tale-telling after the game to actual participation! It is convenient to group together in this section all that material which can be described as creative, including novels and poetry, humorous anecdotes and jokes about the game, cartoons and parodies and the like. This is a particularly rich area and, indeed, many of the earliest writings on the game were in the format of "golfing lays" or poems.

George Robb's *Historical gossip about golf and golfers* (1863) is claimed by some authorities as the first anthology on the game of golf. Others such as the bibliographer Cecil Hopkinson suggest that Horace Hutchinson's *The golfing pilgrim on many links* (1898) was the first collection of essays. Another early work by the so-called poet laureate of golf, Andrew Lang (and some others), was *A batch of golfing papers* (1892). This work, edited by R. Barclay, is a miscellany of poems, essays and humour, and includes 'Dr. Johnson on the links', a narrative piece by Lang on the great English lexicographer's tenuous contact with the game at St. Andrews during his Scottish excursions. Another important early anthology is Miles Bantock's *On many greens* (1901) which includes material selected from journals and newspapers from both sides of the Atlantic. Collected essays from notable golfers and golfing writers are fairly common in the earlier literature, and a typical example is *Golf* (1907) by Henry Seton-Karr and others, who included Hutchinson, Harold Hilton and May Hezlet. Henry Leach's works do not fit comfortably into the previous chapters, and his *Letters of a modern golfer to his grandfather* (1910) was described by his publishers at the time of publication as "a blend of pleasant fiction and practical instruction". Another collection of essays by Leach was published under the title *The happy golfer* (1914). This book had some 400 pages devoted to what the subtitle calls "Some experiences, reflections and a few deductions of a wandering player".

In more recent years other significant collections of essays have appeared. One of quite outstanding merit is Peter Lawless' *The golfer's companion* (1937). This anthology included contributions from the leading golf writers of the day including Bernard Darwin, Robert H.K. Browning and O.B. Keeler. It was also notable for its comprehensive bibliography of golf literature up to 1937. Another work with distinguished contributors was J.S.F. Morrison's *Around golf* (1939), in which essays by Darwin, Henry Longhurst, the playwright Ben Travers and Joyce Wethered appeared. Newton Wethered, the senior member of the golfing Wethered family, published *The perfect golfer* (1931). In this book he speculates, in separate chapters, on the perfect course, the perfect hole and the perfect shot as well as other topics. Chapter 11 sets out to nominate the perfect golf book.

Columnists writing for the major newspapers and journals have long had many of their somewhat transient essays reprinted in book form. Of those that deserve this relative permanence few can equal Bernard Darwin, who was one of the first. The bulk of Darwin's published work is of this genre and dates back to *Tee shots and others*, which appeared in 1911. *Golf from The Times* (1912) contained revised, and sometimes rearranged, articles from Darwin's special contributions to that newspaper which started in

1906. Throughout his subsequent career as a golfing writer Darwin produced a number of other books in the same vein. *A friendly round* (1922), *Second shots* (1930), *Out of the rough* (1932), *Playing the like* (1934) and *Rubs of the green* (1936) consisted mainly of this type of material, both from *The Times* and from the journal *Country Life* for which Darwin also wrote regularly for many years. The last title also included some original essays. Since all Darwin's work is significant, other later essay collections such as *Pack clouds away* (1941), *Golfing by-paths* (1946) and *Golf* (1954) are also worthy of mention. After Darwin's death an anthology, selected by Peter Ryde, was published as *Mostly golf* (1976). This book includes 48 pieces written between 1915 and 1959.

Following in Darwin's footsteps was the excellent Henry Longhurst, whose career encompassed a brief spell as a Member of Parliament, as a successful sporting journalist for the London *Sunday Times* and as a commentator in his later years when golf became a popular televised sport. Longhurst's essay collections included *Golf mixture* (1952), *Round in sixty eight* (1953), which described a round-the-world trip in 68 days during which he played golf on the journey, *Only on Sundays* (1964), *Talking about golf* (1966) and *Never on weekdays* (1968). A posthumous volume of essays by Longhurst, compiled and edited by Mark Wilson and Ken Bowden, was published as *The best of Henry Longhurst* in 1979. These essays were selected from his *Sunday Times* column.

An American writer ranking with Darwin and Longhurst is Herbert Warren Wind. Wind has contributed to various segments of the golfing literature and, like his British counterparts, also wrote regularly for both the golfing and the general press. His essay collections are works of high quality and have rightly received considerable critical acclaim. *The complete golfer* (1954) is one of the great anthologies on the game, and includes five short stories on golf by leading authors. *The lure of golf* (1971), published in the United States as *Herbert Warren Wind's golf book,* is a collection of pieces from the pages of *The New Yorker* and *Sports Illustrated*. In reviewing this work, Henry Longhurst said that "Wind . . . is as outstanding on the American scene as was Bernard Darwin on our own".

Other collections consisting of articles from various magazines include Pat Ward-Thomas' *The long green fairway* (1966) which contains essays selected from *Country Life* and *The Guardian* newspaper. *The best of Golf Digest* (1975) is a collection of varied articles which have appeared in the journal from its inception in 1950 to the year of publication. Another anthology based on items from a journal is Charles Price's *The American golfer* (1964) from the magazine of the same title. Dan Jenkins' unusually titled *Dogged victims of inexorable fate* (1970) is a collection of essays from *Sports Illustrated*.

Several books have appeared with the title of *The golfer's bedside book*. Two of these, appearing in 1965 and 1971, are by Donald Steel. This is certainly confusing for bibliographers since they came from the same publishers. Steel brings together some interesting essays by distinguished contributors. Muir Maclaren's *Golfer's bedside book* (1976) is a splendid anthology on golf in Australia, and other recent anthologies of some distinction are Peter Dobereiner's *Glorious world of golf* (1973) and Michael Hobbs's *Golf for the connoisseur* (1979). The latter work contains an interesting selection of writings dating back to Sir Walter Simpson, and has an index of golfers mentioned in the book which makes it of some value as a reference source.

Some of the general anthologies contain humorous stories on the game. Golf has generated a considerable range of amusing books, with the most prolific writer undoubtedly George Houghton. Although some of Houghton's books are also descriptive and informative, especially on playing golf in unusual locales, most of his work has a distinctive humorous flavour. His *Confessions of a golf addict* (1952) was the first of a series in which the author also provides the cartoons and other illustrative material. In the 1960s, Houghton's "golf addict" turned his attention to golf in various parts of the world, and some of the titles of his books reflect this. *Golf addict among the Irish* (1965), *Golf addict among the Scots* (1967), *Golf addict goes east* (1967) and *Golf addict in gaucho land* (1970) are all typical examples. *Golf addict goes east* describes his experiences playing golf in exotic countries like India, Malaysia, the Philippines and Japan, and *Gaucho land* includes golfing stories based on a South American visit.

Golfing humour, however, dates back to the turn of the century at least, and the ubiquitous Horace G. Hutchinson was one of the earliest writers in this sector with his *After dinner golf* (1896). This book was a collection of amusing essays. Another early writer was Gerald Batchelor with *Golf stories* (1914) which consists of jokes and anecdotes. The British humorous magazine *Punch* was quick to seize on the funny side of golf, and over the years has published several collections of stories and cartoons relating to the game. An early example is Mr. *Punch's golf stories told by his merry men* (1909), and in 1929, E.V. Knox's *Mr. Punch on the links* was also selected from the pages of the journal. A more recent editor, William Davis, produced the *Punch book of golf* (1973) which continued this tradition. Caddies have often been key figures in golfing stories and jokes, and an anthology of stories devoted to their sayings and doings was *Candid caddies* (1935) by Charles Graves and Henry Longhurst.

Important authors such as P.G. Wodehouse, Paul Gallico and Stephen Leacock have all written about golf in a humorous vein. Some of their work is mentioned elsewhere in this chapter, and collections by others have often included pieces by them. One such collection — better than most — is Mervyn Huston's *Great golf humour* (1977) published in Edmonton, Alberta. A collection featuring well-known British writers is Robert Anderson's *A funny thing happened on the way to the clubhouse* (1971) in which many of the stories are based on actual events. The leading magazines such as *Golf Digest* have also produced anthologies of humorous stories such as *Great golf humor from Golf Digest* (1979). Some humorous books are produced with a serious purpose, as is the case with Dick Harris' *How to take the fun out of golf* (1970) which aims to teach course etiquette.

The concept of "gamesmanship", first articulated by Stephen Potter, has not been unknown to generations of golfers keen to win at all costs but without actually cheating. Potter's *Complete golf gamesmanship* (1968) is a minor classic of its type. Somewhat similar in style is Michael Green's *The art of coarse golf* (1967) which is one of a series by the author describing the antics of sportsmen in various games. In all Green's "coarse" books the narrator plays these games more or less to the rules without letting these rules interfere with more important aspects such as winning against long-suffering opponents. Other famous humorists who turned their attention at least briefly to the comic sides of the game of golf are Stephen Leacock in *Why I refuse to play golf* (192?), Charles Schultz with *Snoopy's grand slam* (1972) and W. Heath Robinson in *Humours of golf* (1923). Robinson was a famous illustrator, and his work pioneered what has also become something of a growth industry — the golfing cartoon. Examples of more recent collections include Lawrence Lariar's *You've got me in a hole* (1955) and Peter Davidson's *That's golf* (1979). Davidson includes over 150 drawings of some of the strange and unusual events in golf.

Humorous and other verse has also featured prominently in the literature, and dates back many years. One of the earliest separate publications of poetry is Thomas Marsh's *Blackheath golfing lays* (1875), which was privately published and is, according to Horace G. Hutchinson, mainly of "local and Blackheathian interest". John Somerville's *A foursome at Rye* (1898) consists of a single epic poem of some 60 pages. Other earlier works include Robert Risk's *Songs of the links* (1904) and F.B. Keene's *Lyrics of the links* (1923). This latter work includes a prose (though perhaps not prosaic) definition of golf by David R. Forgan which reads as follows:

"It is a science — the study of a lifetime in which you may exhaust yourself but never your subject. It is a contest, a duel or a mêlée, calling for courage, skill, strategy and self control. It is a test of temper, a trial of honour, a revealer of character. It affords the chance to play the man and act the gentleman. It means getting into God's out-of-doors, getting close to nature, fresh air, exercise, a sweeping away of the mental cobwebs, genuine re-creation of the tired tissues. It is a cure for care — an antidote to worry. It includes companionship with friends, social intercourse, opportunities for courtesy, kindliness and generosity to an opponent. It promotes not only physical health but moral force".

Other poetical volumes include the two parodies on the *Rubaiy-*

at of Omar Khayyam. The first appeared in 1901. This was *Golfer's Rubaiyat* by H.W. Boynton. The second, *The Rubaiyat of a golfer* by J.A. Hammerton, was published in 1946.

Other books which are worthy of brief mention are the golfing joke books which are probably well thumbed by raconteurs looking for a story to tell after a club match or at a golfing function. Many of the best jokes are almost certainly unprintable, even in today's more relaxed and progressive times. Those that are printable appear in volumes such as *One hundred and one great golf jokes and stories* (1968) by Stan McDougal, Ragaway's *The world's worst golf jokes* (1973) and Don Lewis' *After dinner golf* (1976).

Golf fiction is also a fairly plentiful species, though it has to be said that many novels purporting to be about the game use it purely as background. The thriller or detective story in particular has found golf — including golf links and clubhouse — a useful setting for working out its plots. A brief, but excellent, résumé of this sector is provided by Marvin Lachman in an article "Sports and the mystery story: golf" which was reprinted in *The best of the bulletin* (1978). This collection of pieces from the *Golf Collector's Society Bulletin*, edited by Joseph Murdoch, includes many items of historical interest in addition to Lachman's article. One of the more realistic novels of this genre is Angus Macvicar's *Murder at the Open* (1965). Herbert Adams was certainly one of the most prolific, with *Death on the first tee* (1957) a fairly typical example. In some of Adams' novels his detective Roger Bennion conducts his interrogations while playing a round with a suspect! Adams' first book on golfing themes was a collection of 19 short stories, *The perfect round,* published in 1927 and described by him as "tales of golfers, rather than tales of golf".

Of these novels where golf is an integral part of the story an early and classic work which has been reprinted many times is Robert Marshall's *The haunted major* (1902). This novel is based on early St Andrews golfing characters including 'Andra' Kirkaldy. The most recent edition from the Scottish Academic Press appeared in 1973. The United States edition, entitled *The enchanted golf clubs*, was originally published in 1920. Other books with a golfing plot include Horace Hutchinson's early novel *Bert Edward, the golf caddie* (1903) which tells the story of a caddie who became Open Champion.

Another early novel was *John Henry Smith* by F.U. Adams, published in 1905 and subtitled "A humorous romance of outdoor life". Donald McDougall's *Davie* (1977) is believed to be based on the life of Tommy Armour and is one of the few novels where the game of golf is germane to the development of the story line. Earlier in this chapter mention was made of the work of some famous authors whose main contributions were made to other sections of literature but who nevertheless must be considered as writers of importance to golf. P.G. Wodehouse loved the game, and published a number of short stories and some novels which are minor golfing classics. *Heart of a goof* (1926) and *The clicking of Cuthbert* (1922) are two of these. More recently *Golf omnibus* (1973) included over 30 short stories on different, and usually amusing, aspects of the game. Paul Gallico, who started out as a sports journalist before becoming a very successful American novelist, produced a collection of short stories, *Golf is a friendly game,* in 1942. A theme which has recurred in more recent novels published since 1960 is "life on the professional tour". Some of these novels have an authentic setting, and Arthur Pickens' *The golf bum* (1970) and Dan Jenkins' *Dead solid perfect* (1974) are both good examples of these. Herbert Warren Wind's *On the tour with Harry Sprague* (1960) seems to have started this particular fashion.

BIBLIOGRAPHY

ADAMS, Frederick Upham   John Henry Smith: a humorous
    romance of outdoor life.
    New York, Doubleday Page, 1905. 346pp. Early golfing
    novel.

ADAMS, Herbert   The body in the bunker.
    Philadelphia, Lippincott, 1935. 283pp.

– Death on the first tee.
    London, Macdonald, 1957. 192pp.

– The golf house murder.
    Philadelphia, Lippincott, 1933.

– The perfect round: tales of the links.
    London, Methuen, 1927. Second edition 1929. Collection of
    short stories.

ALLISS, Peter   Bedside golf.
    London, Collins, 1980. Golfing anecdotes, with cartoons by
    Bill Tidy.

ALPERT, Hollis, MOTHNER, Ira and SCHONBERG, Harold
    How to play double bogey golf.
    New York, Quadrangle Press, 1965. 177pp. Humour.

ANDERSON, Robert, ed.   A funny thing happened on the way
    to the clubhouse.
    London, A. Barker, 1971. 127pp.

— Heard at the nineteenth: a lighthearted look at the game of golf.
London, S. Paul, 1966. 125pp.

BALL, Brian   Death of a low handicap man.
London, A. Barker, 1974. 224pp. Mystery novel.

BANTOCK, Miles   On many greens: a book of golf and golfers.
New York, Grosset and Dunlap, 1901. 167pp.

BARNETT, Ted   Golf is madness.
Norwalk, Ct, Golf Digest, 1977. 128pp. Ten humorous short stories.

BATCHELOR, Gerald   Golf stories.
London, A. and C. Black, 1914. 131pp. Second edition 1917. Mostly consists of golfing jokes and amusing anecdotes.

BATEMAN, H.M.   Adventures at golf.
London, Methuen, 1923. 50pp. Cartoons.

— H.M. Bateman on golf.
Weybridge, Whitlet Books, 1977. 80pp.

BORDY, Sidney   How to break ninety before you reach it.
New York, William-Frederick Press, 1967. 47pp. Book of humorous verse.

BOX, Sydney   Alibi in the rough.
London, R. Hale, 1977.

BOYNTON, Henry Walcott   Golfer's Rubaiyat.
Chicago, Stone, 1901. 79pp. London, Grant Richards, 1903.

BROWNING, Robert H.K.   The stymie: a miscellany of golfing humour and wit.
Glasgow, Fraser, Asher, 1910. 104pp.

BRUFF, Nancy   The country club.
New York, Bartholomew House, 1969. 339pp. Novel set in a

rich Connecticut county. Much intrigue, sex and similar and not a lot of golf.

CAMPBELL, Patrick   How to become a scratch golfer.
London, Blond, 1963. 144pp. Golf humour.

— Patrick Campbell's golfing book.
London, Blond and Biggs, 1972. 128pp.

CARRELL, Al *and* JANUARY, Don   Golf is a funny game.
New York, Barnes, 1967. 128pp.

CHRISTIE, Agatha   The murder on the links.
London, Hodder and Stoughton, 1923. London, Transworld, 1954. (Paperback edition)

CONNOLLY, Robert   Carnaby Threep's golf class.
Johannesburg, *Sunday Times*, 1971. 52pp. Parody of the Gary Player cartoon instructional strip.

CROSBIE, Provan   Fairways and foul.
London, R. Hale, 1964. 192pp.

CRUICKSHANK, Charles Greig   The Tang murders.
London, R. Hale, 1976.

DARWIN, Bernard   A friendly round.
London, Mills and Boon, 1922. 142pp. Collection of short pieces from *The Times.*

— Golf.
London, Burke, 1954. 222pp. (Pleasures of life series) Includes a bibliography on pages 219-220.

— Golf from The Times: reprint, revised and rearranged, of some articles on golf by *The Times* special contributor.
London, The Times, 1912. 141pp.

— Golfing by-paths.
London, *Country Life,* 1946. 203pp.

— Mostly golf: a Bernard Darwin anthology, edited by Peter Ryde.
London, A. and C. Black, 1976. 198pp.

— Out of the rough.
London, Chapman and Hall, 1932. 336pp.

— Pack clouds away.
London, Collins, 1941. 288pp.

— Playing the like.
London, Chapman and Hall, 1934. 246pp. Book club edition London, Sportsmans Book Club, 1952. Collection of essays from *The Times* and *Country Life*.

— Rubs of the green.
London, Chapman and Hall, 1936. 260pp.

— Second shots: casual talks about golf.
London, Newnes, 1930. 178pp.

— Tee shots and others.
London, Kegan Paul, 1911. 269pp.

DAVIDSON, Peter   That's golf!
Glasgow, Munro-Barr, 1979.

DAVIS, William, *ed.*   The Punch book of golf.
London, Hutchinson, 1973. 112pp.

DOBEREINER, Peter   The glorious world of golf.
London, Hamlyn, 1973. 250pp. New York, McGraw-Hill/ Ridge, 1973. 250pp.

DUKE, Will   Fair prey.
London, Boardman, 1958. 188pp. Features a professional golfer as the detective.

DULACK, Thomas   Pork, or the day I lost the Masters.
New York, Dial Press, 1968. 209pp. Novel about a country "bumpkin" who joins the American professional tour.

DUNN, Seymour   The complete golf joke book.
New York, Stravon Publishers, 1953. 128pp.

DUNNETT, Dorothy   Match for a murderer.
Boston, Houghton Mifflin, 1971. 306pp. Suspense novel.

EVANS, Webster *and* SCOTT, Tom, *comps.*   In praise of golf:
an anthology for all lovers of the game.
London, Muller, 1950. 63pp. Second edition 1955.

FORSE, Harry   The seventy second hole.
Greenfield, Ind, Mitchell-Fleming, 1976. 190pp. Novel.

FROME, David   The murder on the sixth hole.
London, Methuen, 1931. 216pp.

GALLICO, Paul   Golf is a friendly game.
New York, A.A. Knopf, 1942. 274pp.

GLADSTONE, Irving A.   Confessions of a golf duffer in search
of no-fault insurance.
New York, Frederick Fell, 1977. 148pp.

GOLF DIGEST.   Best of *Golf Digest:* the first 25 years.
New York, Simon and Schuster, 1975. 224pp.

— Great golf humor from *Golf Digest.*
Norwalk, Ct, *Golf Digest,* 1979. Includes stories by
P.G. Wodehouse, John Updike, Henry Longhurst and many
others. Also includes many cartoons.

GRAVES, Charles *and* LONGHURST, Henry   Candid caddies.
London, Duckworth, 1935. 120pp. New York, Citadel Press,
1947.

GREEN, Michael   The art of coarse golf.
London, Hutchinson, 1967. 126pp. London, Arrow Books,
1971. 160pp. (Paperback edition)

GREENSHAW, Wayne   The golfer.
Philadelphia, Lippincott, 1967. 219pp.

GRESSWELL, Peter   Week-end golfer.
London, John Murray, 1977. 192pp. An account of a typical
year for an amateur golfer.

GUINEY, David   The Dunlop book of golf.
Lavenham, Suffolk, Eastland Press, 1974. 212pp. Anecdotes,
amazing feats, amusing incidents . . . and more.

HACKETT, Buddy   The truth about golf and other lies.
New York, Doubleday, 1968. 124pp. Golf jokes.

HAMMERTON, J.A.   The Rubaiyat of a golfer.
London, *Country Life,* 1946. 74pp.

HARDCASTLE, Michael   Aim for the flag.
Chicago, Follett, 1969. 192pp. Novel about a "tour"
veteran.

HARRIS, Dick   How to take the fun out of golf.
La Jolla, Ca, Harris and Associates, 1970. 64pp.

HELME, Eleanor E.   Family golf.
London, Dent, 1938. 272pp.

HOBBS, Michael, *ed.*   Golf for the connoisseur: a golfing
anthology.
London, Batsford, 1979. 256pp.

HOUGHTON, George   Addict in bunkerland.
London, *Country Life,* 1962. 103pp. Cartoons.

— Confessions of a golf addict.
London, Museum Press, 1952. 94pp.

— The full confessions of a golf addict.
London, Pelham, 1966. 148pp.

— Golf addict among the Irish.
London, *Country Life,* 1965. 177pp.

— Golf addict among the Scots.
London, *Country Life,* 1967. 136pp.

— Golf addict goes east.
London *Country Life,* 1967. 142pp. Anecdotes, humour
and golfing experiences in India, Thailand, Malaysia,
Singapore, The Philippines, Japan and Hong Kong.

— Golf addict in gaucho land.
London, Pelham, 1970. 198pp. Golf in South America.

— Golf addict invades Wales: the account of a crusade.
London, Pelham Books, 1969. 192pp.

— Golf addict omnibus: the best of George Houghton.
London, *Country Life,* 1966. 305pp. Includes: "Portrait of
a golf addict' 1960; 'I am a golf widow' 1961; and 'Golf
addict strikes again' 1963.

— Golf addict strikes again: the incredible account of a fanatical
golfer who took advice profitably.
London, *Country Life,* 1963. 103pp.

— Golf addict visits the USA.
London, Museum Press, 1955. 85pp.

— Golf addicts galore.
London, *Country Life,* 1968. Cartoons.

— Golf addicts on parade.
London, *Country Life,* 1959. 100pp. Cartoons.

— Golf addicts through the ages.
London, Museum Press, 1956. 86pp.

— Golf on my pillow: midnight letters to a son in foreign parts.
London, S. Paul, 1958. 146pp. London, *Country Life,* 1960.
104pp.

— Golf with a whippy shaft.
New York, Barnes, 1971. 287pp. Collection of items from
earlier Houghton books packaged for the American market.

— Golfers in orbit.
London, Pelham, 1968. 141pp.

— Golfer's treasury: a personal anthology.
London, Newnes, 1964. 208pp.

— How to be a golf addict.
London, Pelham, 1971. 202pp. New York, Transatlantic,
1972.

— Just a friendly: a book of golf addict cartoons.
London, Leslie Frewin, 1973. 96pp.

— More confessions of a golf addict.
London, Museum Press, 1954. 86pp. Second edition 1958.

— Portrait of a golf addict: a monograph in words and pictures.
London, *Country Life,* 1960. 104pp.

— Secret diary of a golf addict's caddie.
London, *Country Life,* 1964. 98pp.

— The truth about golf addicts: an anthology of carefree notes
and drawings.
London, Museum Press, 1957. 194pp. United States edition
entitled Confessions of a golf addict. New York, Simon and
Schuster, 1959. 182pp.

— *and* SIMMONS, Hubert   Golfer's ABC: a golfabet for
addicts.
London, Museum Press, 1953. 56pp.

HUSTON, Mervyn J. *ed.*   Great golf humour: a collection of
stories and articles.
Edmonton, Alberta, Hurtig Publishers, 1977. 287pp.

HUTCHINSON, Horace G.   After dinner golf.
London, Hudson and Kearns, 1896. Collection of humorous
essays.

— Aspects of golf.
Bristol, J.W. Arrowsmith, 1900. 150pp.

— Bert Edward, the golf caddie.
London, John Murray, 1903. 257pp.

— The golfing pilgrim on many links.
London, Methuen, 1898. 287pp.

INGHAM, John, *comp*.   Best golfing jokes.
London, Wolfe, 1969. 63pp.

JAMES, Joe   How to give up golf.
New York, Barnes, and London, Yoseloff, 1970.
106pp. Humour.

— So you're taking up golf.
New York, Barnes, and London, Yoseloff, 1969.
89pp. Humour.

JENKINS, Dan   Dead solid perfect.
New York, Atheneum Press, 1974. 234pp. Novel.

— The dogged victims of inexorable fate.
Boston, Little Brown, 1970. 298pp.

JENNY, Albert   The royal game: stories around a little white
ball.
London, PRM Publishers, 1962. 101pp. Translated from the
German by H. Mitchell.

JONES, Robert 'Bob'   Gulls on the golf course.
Philadelphia, Darrance, 1975. 64pp. Novel.

KEENE, Francis Bowler   Lyrics of the links: poetry, sentiment
and humour of golf.
New York, D. Appleton, and London, Cecil Palmer,
1923. 126pp.

KNOX, E.V., *ed*.   Mr. Punch on the links.
London, Methuen, 1929. 147pp. New York, Rae D. Henkle,
1929. Poems, cartoons and essays selected from *Punch*
magazine.

LACHMAN, Marvin.   "Sports and the mystery story: V, golf"
in The best of the bulletin: a selection of scraps and patches.
(From The armchair detective. Reprinted in *Golf Collector's
Society Bulletin* 1970-1977, 1978. pp.29-32)

LANCASTER, H. Boswell   Ridiculous golf: in story and
verse.
London, Stockwell, 1938. 88pp.

LANG, Andrew *and others*   A batch of golfing papers, edited
by R. Barclay.
London, Simpkin Marshall, 1892. 123pp. New York, M.P.
Mansfield. Miscellany of poems, essays and humour.

— Monifieth golf links bazaar book.
Dundee, John Leng, 1899.

LANGDON, David   How to talk golf: David Langdon's A-Z
glossary of golfing terms.
London, Eyre Methuen, 1975. 80pp. Humorous dictionary
of golf.

LARDNER, Rex   Downhill lies and other falsehoods, or how
to play dirty golf.
New York, Hawthorn, 1973. 152pp. New York, New
American Library, 1976. Humour. (Paperback edition)

LARIAR, Lawrence   Golf and be damned.
New York, Prentice-Hall, 1954. 128pp. London, Hammond,
1956. 128pp. Humour.

— , *ed.*   You've got me in a hole: a collection of the best
golfing cartoons by the foremost comic artists.
New York, Dodd Mead, 1955. 128pp.

LAWLESS, Peter, *ed.*   The golfer's companion.
London, Dent, 1937. 498pp. Second edition 1939.
Contributors include Bernard Darwin, Henry Cotton,
Robert H.K. Browning, A.H. Padgham, Hylton Cleaver,
Eleanor Helme, O.B. Keeler and R.C. Robertson-Glasgow.

LEACOCK, Stephen   Why I refuse to play golf: a story from
"Over the footlights".
London, John Lane, 192?.

LEACH, Henry   The happy golfer: being some experiences, reflections and a few deductions of a wandering player. London, Macmillan, 1914. 414pp.

—, *comp.*   Letters of a modern golfer to his grandfather being the correspondence of Richard Allingham Esq. London, Mills and Boon, 1910. 309pp.

LEWIS, Don   After dinner golf. London, Mowbrays, 1976. 124pp. Golf jokes and anecdotes.

LONGHURST, Henry   The best of Henry Longhurst: on golf and life, compiled and edited by Mark Wilson and Ken Bowden. London, Collins, 1979. 206pp. London, Fontana, 1980. 206pp. (Paperback edition) Anthology of short essays originally written for *The Sunday Times.*

— Golf mixture. London, Werner Laurie, 1952. 204pp. Collection of essays.

— Never on weekdays. London, Cassell, 1968. 182pp. Essays.

— Only on Sundays. London, Cassell, 1964. 260pp.

— Round in sixty eight. London, Werner Laurie, 1953. 174pp.

— Talking about golf. London, Macdonald, 1966. 150pp.

LOOKER, Samuel J.   On the green: an anthology for golfers. London, O'Connor, 1922. 237pp.

LYTTLETON, R.H.   Out-door games: cricket and golf. London, Dent, 1901. 252pp. Pages 130 *et seq.* devoted to golf.

McCUTCHEON, H.   Cover her face. London, Rich and Cowan, 1954. Novel.

McDOUGAL, Stan   One hundred and one great golf jokes
  and stories.
  New York, Citadel Press, 1968. 64pp.

McDOUGALL, Donald   Davie.
  London, Macmillan, 1977. 254pp. New York, St. Martins
  Press. 254pp.

MACLAREN, Muir, *ed*.   The golfer's bedside book.
  Sydney, Reed, 1976. 332pp.

MACVICAR, Angus   Murder at the Open.
  London, J. Long, 1965. 184pp.

— Painted doll affair.
  London, J. Long, 1973.

MAHOOD, *pseud*.   Fore!: forty drawings by Mahood, edited
  by Blos.
  London, Hammond, 1959. 40pp.

MARSH, Thomas   Blackheath golfing lays.
  London (?), The author, 1875. 143pp. Early golfing verse.

MARSHALL, Robert   The haunted major.
  London, Alexander Moring, 1902. 192pp. United States
  edition entitled The enchanted golf clubs, 1920. Several
  later editions (Britain) 1912, 1932, 1937, 1940, 1951 and
  1973. (Edinburgh, Scottish Academic Press) Later US
  editions 1960 and 1963. Classic golf novel.

MARTIN, H.B., *comp*.   Golf yarns: the best things about the
  game of golf.
  New York, Dodd Mead, 1913. 85pp.

MORRISON, J.S.F., *ed*.   Around golf.
  London, A. Barker, 1939. 246pp. Anthology with
  contributions by Bernard Darwin, Joyce Wethered, Henry
  Longhurst, Guy C. Campbell, Ben Travers, C.J.H. Tolley and
  A.P.F. Chapman.

MORRISON, Morie   Life with par.
New York, Doubleday, 1958. 96pp.

MORTON, Cecil   Golf: the confessions of a club secretary.
London, Hammond, 1963. 93pp. Humour.

MOSES, R.J.H.   Fore!
London, Eyre and Spottiswoode, 1937. 146pp. Humorous
miscellany.

NASH, George C.   General Forcursue and Co.: more letters to
the secretary of a golf club.
London, Chatto and Windus, 1936. 213pp.

— Letters to the secretary of a golf club.
London, Chatto and Windus, 1935. 196pp.

— Whelks postbag: still more letters to the secretary of a golf
club.
All three are golf humour.

O'CONNOR, Anthony   Golfing in the green.
London, Martin Brian and O'Keefe, 1979. Description of a
round-Ireland golfing trip.

O'MALLEY, Bill   Fore — and aft.
New York, Barnes, 1969. 76pp. London, Yoseloff, 1969.
Cartoons.

PICKENS, Arthur E.   The golf bum.
New York, Crown Publishers, 1970. 223pp. Novel based on
an idea by Kermit Schafer.

PLIMPTON, George   The bogey man.
New York, Harper and Row, 1968. 306pp. London, A.
Deutsch, 1969. 306pp. London, Hodder Paperbacks, 1970.
284pp (Paperback edition). Book by American television
personality.

POTTER, Stephen   The complete golf gamesmanship.
London, Heinemann, 1968. 177pp. Harmondsworth,
Penguin, 1971. (Paperback edition) 204pp. United States
edition entitled Golfmanship. New York, McGraw-Hill.
1968. 177pp.

PRICE, Charles, *ed.*   The American golfer.
New York, Random House, 1964. 241pp. Anthology selected
from the *American Golfer* magazine.

PUNCH   Mr. Punch's golf stories told by his merry men.
London, Educational Book Co., 1909. 192pp. (Punch's
library of humour no. 19)

QUANTZ, Nancy   Tee party (fore ladies only).
Philadelphia, Whitmore Publishing Co., 1969. 60pp. Cartoons.

RAFTY, Tony *and* SMITH, Terry   Tony Rafty golfers: a
treasury of stars in caricature.
[Australia], John de Deyer, 1975. 192pp.

RAGAWAY, Martin A.   The world's worst golf jokes.
Los Angeles, Price, Stern and Sloan, 1973.

RAMSEY, Tom   How to cheat at golf, or know when your
opponent does.
Melbourne, Southdown Press, 1968. 58pp.

RAY, Ted   Golf: my slice of life.
London, W.H. Allen, 1972. 127pp. Written by leading
British comedian who enjoyed golf.

REYNOLDS, Frank   The Frank Reynolds golf book: drawings
from *Punch*. London, Methuen, 1932. 102pp.

RISK, Robert K.   Songs of the links.
Edinburgh, G.A. Morton, 1904. 48pp. Several later editions.
Poems on golf.

ROBB, George, *comp.*   Historical gossip about golf and golfers.
Edinburgh, J. Hughes, 1863. 58pp.

ROBINSON, Larry *and* GRAHAM, James, *eds.*   Golfer's digest.
Chicago, Golfers Digest Association, 1966. 320pp.

ROBINSON, W. Heath   Humours of golf.
London, Methuen and New York, Dodd Mead, 1923.
50pp. Reprinted London, Duckworth, 1975. Book of golfing
cartoons by leading British illustrator and humorist.

RODRIGO, Robert, *comp.*   The birdie book: a miscellany of
golf.
London, Macdonald, 1967. 219pp. Collection of brief
essays.

SANTEE, Ross   The bar X golf course.
New York, Farrar and Rinehart, 1933. 159pp. Flagstaff,
Arizona, Northland Press, 1971. 89pp. Golf humour from
Arizona.

SCHULTZ, Charles M.   Snoopy's grand slam.
New York, Holt, Rinehart and Winston, 1972.

SCOTT, Tom *and* COUSINS, Geoffrey   The Ind Coope book
of golf.
London, S. Paul, 1965. 144pp. Essays.

— The wit of golf.
London, Leslie Frewin, 1972. 93pp.

SELLECK, Jack *and* BERNARD, Art   Golf is a trap.
New York, Doubleday, 1968. 63pp. Humour.

SETON-KARR, Henry *and others*   Golf.
London, Greening and Co., 1907. 128pp. (Greenings useful
handbook series) Co-authors are Harold Hilton, Harold
Beveridge, T.J. Macnamara, May Hezlet, J.G. McPherson,
Horace G. Hutchinson and S. Muire Fergusson.

SHEEHAN, Larry, *ed.*   Best golf humor from Golf Digest.
New York, Simon and Schuster, 1972. 160pp.

SMARTT, Patrick   Golf grave and gay.
London, S. Paul, 1964. 160pp. Anthology.

SMITH, Garden G.   Side lights of golf.
London, Sisleys, 1907. 153pp.

SOMERVILLE, John   A foursome at Rye.
Rye, J.L. Deacon, 1898. 61pp.

"STANCLIFFE", *pseud.* (i.e. Stanley Clifford)   An astounding
golf match.
London, Methuen, 1914. 312pp.

STANLEY, Louis T.   The book of golf.
London, Parrish, 1960. 147pp.

— The fresh fairways.
London, Methuen, 1949. 220pp. Anthology of articles
previously appearing in the *Field* magazine.

— The golfer's bedside book.
London, Methuen, 1955. 203pp.

— Green fairways.
London, Methuen, 1947. 204pp.

STEEL, Donald, *ed.*   The golfer's bedside book.
London, Batsford, 1965. 240pp. Collection of interesting
essays by some distinguished contributors.

— The golfer's bedside book.
London, Batsford, 1971. 240pp. Contains all new material
and is *not* a second edition of the previously cited title.

STOBBS, John, *comp.*   At random through the green: a
collection of writing about golf.
London, Pelham, 1966. 221pp. (Golfer's library)

STUART, Ian   Sand trap.
London, R. Hale, 1977. Novel.

TAYLOR, Joshua   The lure of the links.
London, Heath Cranton, 1920. 89pp.

TUTTLE, Anthony   Drive for the green.
London, M. Joseph, 1970. 319pp. Novel.

WARD-THOMAS, Pat   The long green fairway.
London, Hodder and Stoughton, 1966. 192pp.

WATSON, Geoffrey James, *comp.*   Off the tee: favourite
golfing stories of the famous.
London, Foulsham, 1963. 127pp.

WETHERED, H. Newton   The perfect golfer.
London, Methuen, 1931. 246pp.

WHEATLEY, Vera   Mixed foursomes: a saga of golf.
London, Thornton Butterworth, 1936. 126pp. A lengthy
poem taking all 126 pages.

WILD, Roland   Golf: the loneliest game.
Vancouver, Mitchell Press, 1969. 129pp. A personal account
of travels in the cause of playing and reporting on golf.
Includes some humorous anecdotes about famous players.

WILDE, Larry   The official golfer's joke book.
Los Angeles, Pinnacle Books, 1977.

WILSON, Henry Leon   So this is golf.
London, John Lane, 1923. 52pp. New York, Cosmopolitan
Book Corp., 1923. 46pp. Golf humour.

WIND, Herbert Warren   The complete golfer.
New York, Simon and Schuster, 1954. 315pp. London,
Heinemann, 1954. 398pp. One of the great anthologies
on golf.

— The lure of golf.
London, Heinemann, 1971. 317pp. United States edition
entitled Herbert Warren Wind's golf book. New York,
Simon and Schuster, 1971. 317pp. Anthology of essays from
The New Yorker and *Sports Illustrated.*

— On the tour with Harry Sprague.
New York, Simon and Schuster, 1960. 94pp. Novel.

WODEHOUSE, P.G.   The clicking of Cuthbert.
London, Jenkins, 1922. 256pp. United States edition
entitled Golf without tears. New York, G.H. Doran, 1924
330pp. Collection of short stories.

— Golf omnibus: thirty one golfing short stories.
London, Barrie and Jenkins, 1973. 467pp. New York, Simon
and Schuster, 1974. Published originally in the United States
as Wodehouse on golf. New York, Doubleday Doran, 1940.
844pp.

— Heart of a goof.
London, Jenkins, 1926. 314pp. Harmondsworth,
Penguin, 1963. (Paperback edition) United States edition
entitled 'Divots'. New York, G.H. Doran, 1927.

CHAPTER FIVE

THE
GOLF BUSINESS

Golf today, like many other sports, is big business. In Great Britain alone, it is estimated that there are some 1.4 million active golfers, and recent market research indicates that they spent in the region of £140 million on golf equipment and clothing in 1979. In the United States of America over 10 million golfers are claimed; while even in European countries which are not so addicted to the game increasing figures are shown. 1978 figures obtained from within the industry suggest that some 200,000 golfers play on nearly 600 courses in the countries of Western Europe alone, and other advanced countries such as Japan, Australia, South Africa and New Zealand also have a high golfing population. The millions of pounds spent on equipment and clothing is not the only economic aspect since improved living standards and increased leisure time enable more people to travel to play on different courses in their own countries and abroad. The link with tourism generally is therefore very strong. Many more people now depend on the game for their livelihood. These are not only the professional players but many in teaching, administration, recreation planning and management, course design and maintenance, production and marketing of equipment and apparel, catering and the other elements of tourism mentioned already.

This chapter considers the sources of information on these aspects, and identifies key documents relating to them. There are obviously close links with Chapter 7 which provides information on the organisational sources, since some of these organisations are responsible, either directly or indirectly, for some of the publications listed. Coverage in this chapter starts with the planning and provision of facilities. It also includes selected materials on golf course design, layout and maintenance, and on all aspects of golf club administration and management. The limited literature on equipment production and marketing is also examined. Finally, the chapter deals with the considerable literature on "where to play". There is extensive coverage of the guides to courses and resorts in Great Britain and in other countries.

The role of governments in the planning and provision of recreational facilities is a relatively recent phenomenon although there are plenty of examples of involvement by municipalities and local governments in the provision of golf courses. Nevertheless it is fair to say that only in recent years has central government in the United Kingdom become interested in planning the provision of sports facilities. The setting up of the Sports Council, and the creation of a minister responsible for sport within the large Department of the Environment, have provided considerable new impetus. Considerable research into existing facilities has been undertaken and recommendations have been made for improving facilities to cope with the growth of interest in the game. In Britain golf is one of the fastest growing sports, and many courses, especially those near to the main urban centres, are very crowded or prohibitively expensive. The Sports Council's report *Provision for sport* (1972) looked at golf as well as indoor sports centres and swimming pools in the national context. Some earlier work had been done by some of the regional sports councils which are linked to the national body. Other studies have been carried out by local authorities themselves. Typical of these are the South Western Sports Council's *Major recreation survey Devon: golf courses 1971* and an early report by the Northern Council for Sport and Recreation which originally appeared in 1967 and has since been revised and updated as *Golf in the northern region* (1978). A national survey was carried out for the Department of Education and Science by two researchers from the University of Glasgow. The resulting report was *Study of golf course provision in Britain* (1969) which, although it does not appear to have been fully published, is available in several relevant libraries. Other examples of studies include the Sports Council for Northern Ireland's *Existing facilities — golf* (1978?) which lists the golf clubs in the province by district council areas and gives club membership information. In Scotland the Department of Recreation and Leisure of the Lothian Regional Council has produced *Golf: an interim strategy for provision in the Lothian Region* (1978). This area includes some of the more historic and famous golf courses on which many golfing tourists play. There is also a

140

high percentage of golfers among the local population because of strong local traditions.

The provision of the considerable amounts of land required for golf has been the subject of a number of reports and studies. In 1975 the Centre for Advanced Land Use Studies at the University of Reading published the proceedings of a conference held in the previous year, under the title *Land for leisure*. Speakers at this conference included the director of the Golf Development Council, leading golf architects, property developers and representatives of local authorities and the Sports Council. The Golf Development Council, which provides advice direct to the Sports Council, has also published relevant information including the recent *Reclamation of derelict lands for golf* (1980) which was written by the leading golf course architect J. Hamilton Stutt. This is an attempt to overcome the land shortage, especially in or near urban centres, and also to create environmental improvement by utilising colliery slag heaps, open cast coal sites, marshland, sand and gravel pits and refuse disposal areas as new golf courses. The Golf Foundation, which is mainly concerned with the promotion of the game amongst the young, has also produced literature on this topic. *Making room for golf* (1964) is somewhat out of date now but is still useful on the basic elements of providing adequate playing facilities. Other planning approaches are discussed in the professional planning literature from time to time and in reports from academic planning institutes. Tom Jamieson's "Golf – a handicap for planners" which appeared in the *Journal of the Royal Town Planning Institute* in May 1973 is an example of the former, while

A.J. Veal's *Sport and recreation in England and Wales* published by the Centre for Urban and Regional Studies at Birmingham University typifies the latter.

In the United States much planning information is provided by the National Golf Foundation. The objectives and activities of the Foundation are described in Chapter 7. Their *Golf facilities in the United States* is a brief statistical report, regularly brought up to date, which gives the number of golfers and courses on a state-by-state basis. Other reports by this body include *Availability of public courses in US metropolitan areas* (1977) which covers the 259 largest conurbations, and the very substantial *Planning information for private and daily fee golf clubs* which is updated annually and includes national growth statistics. This volume also includes information on course design and maintenance, gives job descriptions of key personnel involved in golf course management, and much more besides.

The municipal golf course sector is covered by *Municipal golf course operational data* (latest edition 1979) which is based on a national survey of courses. It gives separate figures for nine and 18 hole courses. *Senior citizens and golf*, also by the NGF, profiles three successful senior citizen golf programmes, a sector where there is much interest and considerable investment. The National Recreation and Parks Association produced a guide for American local authorities on the development and operation of public golf courses in 1964. This was Cook and Holland's pamphlet *Public golf courses,* which was issued as Management Aid Bulletin number 33.

Golf course architecture is also a subject with an extensive literature. Some of the earliest writings on the topic are subsumed in the early manuals by leading professionals of the turn of the century. At that time the design, layout and maintenance of the course was part of their responsibility, and many of them were highly talented in this connection. We have mentioned already Willie Park's *The game of golf* (1896), the first book by a professional golfer, which included much on course construction. James Braid also became a leading golf course architect in his later days. As design specialists became involved, books devoted particularly to greenkeeping and course layout started to appear. One of the first was edited by Horace G. Hutchinson. This was *Golf greens and greenkeeping* (1906) which had contributions by experts on the different types of soils on which golf was played in Great Britain. Martin H.F. Sutton, of the grass seed company

142

Sutton and Sons, published *Layout and upkeep of golf courses and putting greens* in 1906, and in 1912 he edited an important early work, *The book of the links,* which had contributions from various experts. Although somewhat dated, many of these earlier works have remained of considerable interest. Colt and Alison's *Some essays on golf course architecture* (1920) is one of these, as is Dr. A. Mackenzie's *Golf architecture* (1920). Wethered and Simpson's *The architectural side of golf* (1929) is widely regarded by many experts as a classic book on golf course construction. Two relatively early American works which have remained of value are Robert Hunter's *The links* (1926) and George C. Thomas' *Golf architecture in America* (1927). The latter is a quite outstanding book on its subject.

Two more recent pamphlets produced in the 1970s — one from each side of the Atlantic — are the National Golf Foundation's *Golf course design* and the Golf Development Council's *Elements of golf course layout and design.* Both are 20-page introductions to the subject suitable for, and aimed at, local authorities and developers who have little or no previous knowledge. The GDC booklet includes a list of suggested equipment required to maintain both nine and 18 hole courses when established. The Urban Land Institute of Washington D.C. produced a useful document in its Technical Bulletin series. *Golf course developments* (1974) by Rees L. Jones and Guy L. Rando is well illustrated with site plans for various layouts, and is primarily aimed at property developers and the golf course architects working for them. Other useful and practical manuals include M.H. Ferguson's *Building golf holes for good turf management* (1968) published by the United States Golf Association, and Joseph Finger's *Business end of building or rebuilding a golf course* (1972) which is particularly good on the financial aspects of this operation. The National Golf Foundation's illustrated guide *Planning and building the golf course* (1977) includes brief information on site selection, soils, power and water availability, and also costs. The history of golf course architecture is covered in Gary L. Sorenson's *The architecture of golf* (1976) which also has much to say on current practice, and includes a bibliography on the subject.

The particular problems of municipal golf operations are exhaustively covered, insofar as American practices are concerned, in the National Golf Foundation's *Organising and operating municipal golf courses.* This manual is regularly brought up to date, and the 1979 edition contains 466 pages. It includes case histories of successful municipal golf operations, and provides information on planning procedures, finance, maintenance, the golf shop, public relations, and the problems of public course golf clubs. There appear to be no British counterparts of many of the Foundation's publications. Some examples of specialist guides include *Golf driving range manual* (1978), *The par-3 and executive golf course manual* (1977) and the *Miniature putting course manual* (1978).

Much of the technical information on turfgrass culture is produced in Great Britain by the Sports Turf Research Institute at Bingley in West Yorkshire. Further information on its services and activities is given in Chapter 7. The director of the Institute, J.R. Escritt, is one of the foremost authorities on turf, and has produced several recent books on the topic. These include *The ABC of turf culture* (1978) and *Lawns* (1979). Other publications originating from the Institute include *Turfgrass diseases* (1979), *Identification of grasses in non-flowering condition* (1962) by David Clouston, and *Sports ground construction — specifications* (1975) published by the National Playing Fields Association (NPFA). Other useful texts include a further pamphlet from the NPFA, *Sports ground maintenance* (1978), and Martin Sutton's *Lawns and sports grounds,* of which the 17th edition appeared in 1962. Some American books are Piper and Oakley's *Turf for golf courses* (1917), claimed as the first on the subject and still recognised as a very useful practical guide. John Madison's companion works *Practical turfgrass management* and *Principles of turfgrass culture* both appeared in 1971, and two other substantial reference works are James Beard's *Turfgrass science and culture* (1973) and Hanson and Juska's *Turfgrass science* (1969). A brief but authoritative booklet aimed at the golf professional is William Knoop's *Golf professional's guide to turfgrass maintenance* published by the Professional Golfers' Association of America. It includes a complete glossary of terms and a useful bibliography for further reading. Murray's *Greenkeeping in South Africa* (1932) is a collection of reprinted articles from the journal *South African Golf* and is, as the sub-title states, "A treatise on scientific methods for the establishment and maintenance of turf for sporting purposes. . . ".

There are many fewer sources of information on the specifics of clubhouse, as opposed to course, design. Architect Clifford Wendehack produced a useful book, *Golf and country clubs,* in 1929 in which there were only 50 pages of text to some 157 plates. This work gave valuable information on requirements for the planning and construction of clubhouses. Much more up to date is the National Golf Foundation's *Planning the golf clubhouse* (1977) which gives details of the space required for different facilities related to club membership size. The Foundation's *Golf operations handbook* (1979) provides a valuable guide to all aspects of club and course management and is well indexed which greatly increases its value as a reference tool. Management and organisation of the golf professional's shop is also a topic on which the literature is totally American. The United States Professional Golfers' Association, with its large membership of club professionals, provides considerable information and advice in this very practical area. Kent Cayce's *The PGA book of golf shop policies and procedures* (1980) discusses all aspects of shop management, while *Golf shop merchandising* (197?) consists of current articles extracted from the journal literature describing new equipment and apparel available. Another authoritative manual is the National Golf Foundation's *The professional golf shop* (1977) which covers shop design, merchandising, repairs, golf cars, caddies and other topics.

Golfing equipment is an area in which much of the most significant data are held by the companies operating in the market. Much of this information is confidential, though from time to time it is made more widely available through market research firms operating in this sector. A British firm specialising in the leisure and tourism field is MEW Research, headed by Marion E. Wertheim. Her firm is particularly interested in the golf business and conducts a regular *Survey of British golfers* from which data can be purchased. The survey covers the volume and value of the market for golf balls, clubs, clothing, shoes, gloves, bags and trolleys, brand share information for each product group, image ratings for all leading equipment suppliers, place of purchase data, purchasing influences, readership of leading golfing magazines and golf holiday-taking habits, attitudes and expenditure. A brief pamphlet *The British golf market* was distributed by the firm in 1979. A reference guide for sports marketing is Richard A. Lipsey's *Sportsguide for individual sports* (1980). This volume covers golf as one of a number of major individual sports such as tennis, squash and badminton. It includes information on the major (American) manufacturers, associations and organisations, consumer media, trade shows, events, sources of market data and relevant publications. It features a general index, a master listing of manufacturers, and an executive directory.

The complete guide to golfing equipment (1975) was published by the American *Consumer Guide Magazine* which is a commercial organisation. In Britain the most recent independent tests on golf equipment were carried out in the 1960s by the non-commercial and independent Consumers' Association, and are consequently very much out of date. *Which* magazine carried reports on golf bags in January 1967 and on golf balls in June of the same year. Design of early golf clubs was mentioned in the historical chapter, where Henderson and Stirk's superb recent book *Golf in the making* was listed. Modern golf clubs are the subject of Ralph Maltby's *Golf club design, fitting, alterations and repair* (1974) which has been described as "the definitive book on the design and construction of the . . . golf club". Maltby's *Golf club repair in pictures* (1978) shows step-by-step procedures on the repair of the clubs, and is aimed at the club professional. Also aimed at that market by the PGA of America is Harley Coster's pamphlet on *Golf car policy and economics* (197?). This is a subject of considerable interest in the United States, but the relative scarcity of these vehicles on British golf courses means that such a document is of little interest in the United Kingdom.

To complete the material covered by this chapter it is necessary to examine the very considerable amount of information on golf courses. In particular the growth of golf-based tourism on a world-wide scale has generated a good deal of material in this area. It is of interest to see many earlier works dating back to times when travel, even within one country, was not as widespread as it is today, partly for economic reasons and partly because most people had considerably less leisure time at their disposal.

Some directories of golf clubs, such as the list compiled and annually updated by the Data Research Group under the title *United Kingdom golf clubs,* are primarily for commercial purposes to provide mailing list addresses, but the vast majority in this sector are targeted at the golfer himself. Some give basic factual information on the club including name, address, type of course, length of course, whether visitors may play, and in some cases the green fees. Others are much more selective, including only a limited number of chosen courses which the author has personally enjoyed playing. Yet others are both descriptive and works of genuine literary merit.

Examples of the gazetteer approach include Ken Bowden's *The golf gazetteer* (1968), *Golf Digest's Rand McNally golf course guide* (1966), which lists over 4,200 American golf courses, and the much older and quaintly dated *Golf clubs of the Empire* (1929) edited by T.R. Clougher. Tom Scott's *AA guide to golf in Britain* (1977) has over 400 pages, and includes details of over 1,500 golf courses where visitors are welcome. The international dimension first became significant in the mid-1960s when cheaper air travel and package holidays made their presence felt. The airlines themselves saw the value of guides to golf courses in tourist areas, and one of the first publications from this source was British European Airways' *Golf in the sun* (1965). This has been brought up to date several times since that date, and has been considerably expanded to include additional countries outside Europe. One of the recent issues offered information on golf in Europe, the Mediterranean, Bermuda, the Caribbean, West Indies, South Africa and Thailand, and included contributions from some of the leading golfing writers including Peter Alliss and Peter Dobereiner. An American counterpart, *Golf – new horizons,* was produced for Pan-American Airways by Gene Sarazen and Peter McLean in 1966. This volume includes details of courses in 51 countries. Other international directories include *Great golf courses of the world* (1974) by William H. Davis and the editors of *Golf Digest.* This has been described as "a magnificent book" by Joseph Murdoch, the golfing bibliographer extraordinary, and it contains information on over 900 courses world-wide. Another similar work which also includes much basic travel and cost information is Robert Scharff's *Great golf courses you can play* (1974), produced in collaboration with the journal *Golf Magazine.* Pat Ward-Thomas' *The world atlas of golf* (1976) is also a splendidly produced work, as is Sir Peter Allen's *Famous fairways* (1968) which looks particularly at championship courses in Britain and overseas.

More restricted, but equally valuable, are those whose horizons are, of necessity, more limited. These are the local guides restricted to country, state (as in the US), or county. Such guides have a lengthier history than the previous category, and since Scotland is the home of golf it would be appropriate to start with some of those relating to that country. Peter Baxter's *Golf in Perth and Perthshire* dates back to 1899, while more recent guides include Henry Cotton's *Golfing in Scotland at 100 holiday resorts* (1936) and *Golf courses of Scotland* (1974) by Andy Black.

Black's book divides Scotland into four broad regions, giving all the usual basic information on facilities at each of the courses listed. There are no maps or indexes to this work, which does reduce its value as a reference tool. The Scottish Tourist Board, conscious of the contribution made to the Scottish economy by tourists wishing to play the famous Scottish courses, also produces a directory, *Scotland, home of golf,* which is revised regularly. Some of the earlier editions of this work included articles on various aspects of Scottish golf, but this feature seems to have been dropped. One unusual, and therefore interesting, book is Rod McLeod's *St. Andrews Old* (1970) which describes how 12 leading professional golfers tackled different holes on the famous Old Course at St. Andrews.

It is no surprise to find that Horace G. Hutchinson, who pioneered in so many areas of the golfing literature, should also be responsible for the first book of this type to be published. This was *Famous golf links* (1891) which mainly described British courses but also included a chapter on golf in Canada. Hutchinson edited the work which included contributions from Andrew Lang, H.S.C. Everard and T.R. Clark. *British golf links* (1897) is another classic work by the same author, and provides short accounts of the leading golf links in Britain at the time. Bernard Darwin's important and valuable *Golf courses of the British Isles* appeared originally in 1910 with a second edition under the slightly changed title of *The golf courses of Great Britain* being published in 1925. Darwin, and E.P. Leigh-Bennett, also produced some commissioned work for the railway companies, who in the 1920s and 1930s saw the possibilities of encouraging people to travel for golf in the same way as the airlines hit on a similar idea in the sixties and seventies. Darwin's *A round of golf on the London and North Eastern Railway* (1924) drew attention to those courses in the east and north of England and Scotland, while Leigh-Bennett's books for the Southern Railway were *Some friendly fairways* (1930) and *Southern golf* (1935). Another early work was Josiah Newman's *Guide to London golf* (1913) which claimed to provide a concise guide to recognised golf clubs within 25 miles of Charing Cross (generally used as a marker for the centre of London). This particular locality has more recently been covered by Tom Scott's *Sixty miles of golf around London* (1975) which itself stems from earlier books published in the 1930s by the now defunct golfing journal *Fairway and Hazard*. It gradually widened its scope as road networks improved and car ownership became more widespread.

Many county guides were published, particularly in the years immediately following World War II, and the author of many of these was Robert H.K. Browning. These guides, and many others devoted to a single golf club, were produced by the Golf Clubs Association. In addition to giving current details on courses and club facilities they also included some elements of club history. Other rather personalised guides to British golf courses include George Houghton's *Addict's guide to British golf* (1959), which is a county-by-county pictorial directory. Frank Pennink has also produced several books of interest starting with *Golf* (1952), in which he looks at 30 courses, *Golfer's companion* (1962), covering 128 courses in Great Britain and Ireland, and *Frank Pennink's choice of golf courses* (1976), which is based on the *Golfer's companion*. Leonard Claughton Darbyshire's *Go golfing in Britain* (1961) concentrates on 25 famous seaside courses. Seaside golf is often seen as synonymous with British golf by overseas players and, although this presents a distorted picture of the game in Britain, it is true that many of the most famous and difficult courses are to be found on the coasts.

General guides to British golf courses include Donald Steel's *Golf course guide to the British Isles* which is now in its fifth edition and is a well-established and generally reliable work. It is arranged by broad geographical areas, and includes access information, though the later editions, for cost reasons presumably, have dispensed with the useful coloured maps. Sir Peter Allen's *Play the best courses* (1973) describes 104 major golfing venues and is well illustrated. Some of the material included is to be found in Allen's earlier work, already quoted, *Famous fairways* (1968). Both Allen's books include brief, but useful, bibliographies. A useful guide to Irish golf courses is Oliver Weldon's *Golfing in Ireland* (1970).

Golf in America is equally well documented. One phenomenon which is typically American is the golf resort. Dick Miller's *America's greatest golf resorts* (1977) identifies the top 20 and probably the most expensive of these. A useful *Golfer's atlas* produced by the Professional Golfers' Association of America, presumably for its own members, covers most of the golf courses in the USA showing how to get there and giving the names of the resident professionals. Another guide to golf resorts is Harry Baron's *Golf resorts of the USA* (1967) which covers some 100 resorts, 350 independent courses and 150 municipal facilities in the United States, Bermuda and the Caribbean. *Golfing America*

(1958) by E.A. Hamilton and Charles Preston is a pictorial tour of some American courses. Guides to the courses of particular states include Kent C. Myers' *Golf in Oregon* (1977), *The golfer's guide to Florida courses* (1973) by J.T. Garrity and *Great golf holes of Hawaii* published by John Morris and Leonard Cobb in New Zealand in 1977. Detailed guides to more specific localities include *Fairways: a detailed graphic description of all Los Angeles City and county-operated golf courses* (1967) and *Golf on the peninsula* (1973) in which Frank C. Pollard describes the 12 courses on the Monterey peninsula in California.

Great golf holes of New Zealand (1971) by the Morris and Cobb team responsible for the book on Hawaii mentioned above is an excellent book. Harold Henning, the well-known South African professional, has produced a guide to golf courses in the Republic of South Africa and Zimbabwe under the title *Driving around Southern Africa with Harold Henning* (1974). The continent of Europe has had guides to its golf courses which pre-date the packaged tourist and airline interests. The *Annuaire des golfs de France et du Continent* reached its 17th edition in 1950. This reference work listed golf clubs in 15 different countries on the mainland of Europe. More recent, and aimed more directly at the US tourist when the dollar was all-powerful, is Saul Galin's *Golf in Europe* (1967) which is a guide to some 200 of the best golf courses. More specific in its choice of countries is *Holiday golf in Spain and Portugal* (1970) by Michael Gedye. A number of specialist companies have entered this lucrative sector of the tourist market since that date. Typical of their promotion efforts is *Eurogolf: your second golf club*, which is a guide to European golf courses and appears at fairly regular intervals.

BIBLIOGRAPHY

ALLEN, Peter   Famous fairways: a look at the world of championship courses.
London, S. Paul, 1968. 164pp.

— Play the best courses: great golf in the British Isles.
London, S. Paul, 1973. 264pp.

ANNUAIRE des golfs de France et du continent.
Paris, Paris Vendôme, 17th edition 1950.

BARON, Harry   Golf resorts of the USA.
New York, New American Library, 1967. 335pp. New York, Signet Books, 1968. 352pp. (Paperback edition)

BAUER, Aleck   Hazards: the essential elements in a golf course without which the game would be tame and uninteresting.
Chicago, Toby Rubovits, 1913. 61pp.

BAXTER, Peter   Golf in Perth and Perthshire: traditional, historical and modern.
Perth, Hunter, 1899. 184pp.

BEARD, James B.   Turfgrass science and culture.
Englewood Cliffs, NJ, Prentice-Hall, 1973. 658pp.

BELFAST TOURIST INFORMATION CENTRE   Golfing in Ulster.
London, Office of the Ulster Agent, 1963. 100pp.

BLACK, Andy   Golf courses of Scotland.
London, Macdonald and Jane's, 1974. 130pp.

BOWDEN, Ken, *comp*.   The golf gazetteer.
Walton-on-Thames, The author, 1968. 224pp.

BRITISH EUROPEAN AIRWAYS CORPORATION   Golf in
the sun, 1965.
See entry under GEDYE, M.

BROWNING, Robert H.K.   Golf in the Channel Islands.
London, Golf Clubs Association. Eighth edition 1973.
24pp.

— Golf in Cornwall.
London, Golf Clubs Association, 1952. 88pp.

— Golf in Gloucestershire.
London, Golf Clubs Association, 1953. 54pp.

— Golf in the Isle of Man.
London, Golf Clubs Association, 1973. 20pp.

— Golf in Surrey.
London, Golf Clubs Association, 1973. 80pp.

— Golf in Sussex.
London, Golf Clubs Association, 1972. 60pp.

— Golf on the Lancs. coast.
London, Golf Clubs Association, 1956. 56pp.

CAYCE, Kent   The PGA book of golf shop policies and
procedures.
Lake Park, Fl, Professional Golfers' Association of America,
1980.

CENTRE FOR ADVANCED LAND USE STUDIES   Land for
leisure, edited by A.W. Davidson and J.E. Leonard.
Reading, The centre, 1975. 49pp. (Property studies in the
United Kingdom and overseas no. 6) Proceedings of a conference held in October 1974. Speakers: G.A. McPartlin,

Golf Development Council; R.C. Williams, Cheshire Planning Department; H.J. Lewis, Southern Sports Council; W.R. Hillary, Strutt and Parker; F.W. Hawtree, Hawtree and Son; and M.F. Bonallack, Miller Buckley Golf Services Ltd.

CLAUGHTON DARBYSHIRE, Leonard   Go golfing in Britain: a hole-by-hole survey of 25 famous seaside courses.
London, *Sunday Times,* 1961. 75pp.

CLOUGHER, T. R., *ed.*   Golf clubs of the Empire.
London, Clougher Corporation, 1929. 512pp. Third year of the *Golfing annual.*

CLOUSTON, David   Identification of grasses in non-flowering condition.
Bingley, Sports Turf Research Institute, 1962.

COLT, H.S. *and* ALISON, C.H.   Some essays on golf course architecture, with contributions by Dr. A. Mackenzie, Horace G. Hutchinson, John L. Low and others.
London, *Country Life* and Newnes, 1920. 69pp. New York, Scribners, 1920.

CONSUMER GUIDE MAGAZINE, *ed.*   Complete guide to golfing equipment.
New York, New American Library, 1975.

COOK, Walter L *and* HOLLAND, Roy   Public golf courses: a guide to their development and operation.
Washington DC, National Recreation and Park Association, 1964. 36pp. (Management aid bulletin no. 33).

COSTER, Harley   Golf car policy and economics.
Lake Park, Fl, Professional Golfers' Association of America, 197?. 47pp.

COTTON, Henry   Henry Cotton's guide to golf in the British Isles.
Manchester, Cliveden Press, 1959. 125pp. Describes 57 of Britain's finest courses.

— *and* WHITE, Jack   Golfing in Scotland at 100 holiday resorts.
London, Ed Burrow, 1936. 124pp.

CRIPPLEGATE PRINTING CO. LTD.   Golf par excellence, 1980.
Edenbridge, Kent, Cripplegate, 1980. 160pp. Details of 150 European golf courses. For the golfing tourist.

DARWIN, Bernard   Golf courses of the British Isles.
London, Duckworth, 1910. 253pp. Second edition entitled The golf courses of Great Britain. London, Cape, 1925.

— A round of golf on the London and North Eastern Railway.
York, Ben Johnson Co., 1924. 153pp.

DATA RESEARCH GROUP   United Kingdom golf clubs.
Amersham, Bucks., The group, annually updated. Various paging.

DAVIS, William H. *and* editors of GOLF DIGEST   Great golf courses of the world.
New York, Harper and Row, 1974. 278pp.

DELLOR, Ralph   British golf courses: a guide to courses and clubs in the British Isles.
London, Lansdowne Publications, 1974. 439pp.

DICKINSON, Patric   A round of golf courses: a selection of the best eighteen.
London, Evans Brothers, 1951. 159pp.

ESCRITT. J.R.   ABC of turf culture.
London, Kaye and Ward, 1978. 248pp.

— Lawns.
Sevenoaks, Kent, Teach Yourself Books, 1979. 113pp.

EUROGOLF: your second golf club.
London, Eurogolf Ltd., 1977. 265pp. Guide to European golf courses. Serial publication probably annual.

FAIRWAYS: a detailed, graphic description of all Los Angeles
city and county-operated golf courses.
Los Angeles, Format Publications, 1967. 164pp.

FERGUSON, M.H.   Building golf holes for good turf management.
New York, United States Golf Association, 1968. 55pp.

FINGER, Joseph S.   The business end of building or rebuilding
a golf course.
Houston, Texas, The author, 1972. 47pp.

GALIN, Saul   Golf in Europe: a guide to 200 best golf courses.
New York, Hawthorn Books, 1967. 281pp.

GARRITY, J.T.   The golfer's guide to Florida courses.
New York, Cornerstone, 1973. 191pp.

GEDYE, Michael, *ed.*   Golf in the sun: a recommendation of
some of the best places to stay throughout Europe,
the Mediterranean, Bermuda, the Caribbean, West Indies, South
Africa and Thailand.
London, Fairgreen Publications, annual. Continues the
publication by British European Airways Corporation, *q.v.*

— Holiday golf in Spain and Portugal.
London, Fairgreen Publications, 1970. 126pp.

GLASGOW UNIVERSITY. Department of Social and Economic
Research   Study of golf course provision in Britain:
a report for submission to the Department of Education and
Science by D.C. Nicholls and D.W. Massey.
Glasgow, University of Glasgow, 1969. 37pp.

GOLF DEVELOPMENT COUNCIL   Elements of golf course
layout and design.
London, Golf Development Council, 197?. 20pp.

GOLF DIGEST   Rand McNally golf course guide.
Chicago, Rand McNally, 1966. 200pp. Lists over 4,200
United States golf courses.

GOLF DIGEST   Traveler's guide to golf.
    Norwalk, Ct, Golf Digest, 1976. 192pp.

GOLF FOUNDATION LTD.   Making room for golf.
    London, Golf Foundation, 1964. 52pp. Discusses the
    problems of providing adequate playing facilities with notes
    on procedures.

GOLF professional's handbook of business: the best of pro
    business practices as contributed by professionals.
    Providence, RI, United States Rubber Company, 1932.
    98pp.

GORDON, Hugh M.   Repair your own golf clubs.
    Richmond, Va, Dietz Press, 1959. 40pp.

GRAFFIS, Herb, ed.   Planning the professional's shop.
    Chicago, National Golf Foundation, 1951. 50pp.

GUIDE to golf courses in the U.K.
    London, IPC, 1973. 274pp.

HAMILTON, Edward, A. and PRESTON, Charles, eds.
    Golfing America.
    New York, Doubleday, 1958. 128pp. Pictorial tour of some
    American courses.

HANSON, A.A. and JUSKA, F.V., eds.   Turfgrass science.
    Madison, Wisconsin, American Society of Agronomy, 1969.
    715pp.

HENNING, Harold   Driving around Southern Africa with
    Harold Henning.
    Transvaal, J.M. Samuel, 1974. 96pp.

HOPE, Frank   Turf culture: a complete manual for the
    groundsman.
    Poole, Blandford Press, 1978. 293pp.

HOUGHTON, George   An addict's guide to British golf: a
    county-by-county pictorial directory.
    London, S. Paul, 1959. 323pp.

HUBBARD, Charles Edward   Grasses.
Harmondsworth, Penguin Books, 1968.

HUNTER, Robert   The links.
New York, Scribners, 1926. 163pp. Early book on
golf course architecture.

HUTCHINSON, Horace G., *ed.*   British golf links: a short
account of the leading golf links of the United Kingdom.
London, J.S. Virtue, 1897. 331pp.

— Famous golf links.
London, Longmans Green, 1891. 201pp.

— *ed.*   Golf greens and greenkeeping; with contributions by
specialists in dealing with the different types of soils on which
golf is played in Great Britain.
London, *Country Life,* 1906. 219pp. (Country Life library
of sports) New York, Scribners, 1906.

JAMIESON, Tom   Golf — a handicap for planners?
Journal of the Royal Town Planning Institute, volume 59(5),
May 1973, pp.215-218.

JENKINS, Dan   Sports Illustrated's best 18 golf holes in
America.
New York, Delacorte Press, 1966. 160pp.

JONES, Rees L. *and* RANDO, Guy L.   Golf course
developments.
Washington DC, Urban Land Institute, 1974. 112pp.
(Technical bulletin series no. 70).

JONES, Robert 'Bob'   British golf odyssey.
Monterey, Ca, Angel Press, 1977. 152pp. Comments of an
American golfer touring British golf courses.

KNOOP, William E.   The golf professional's guide to turfgrass
maintenance.
Lake Park, Fl, Professional Golfers' Association of America
197? 20pp.

LEIGH-BENNETT, E.P.   An errant golfer.
London, Hurst and Blackett, 1929. 288pp.

— Some friendly fairways.
London, Southern Railway, 1930. 57pp.

— Southern golf.
London, Southern Railway, 1935. 167pp.

LIPSEY, Richard A., *ed.*   Sportsguide for individual sports.
Detroit, Gale Research Company, 1980. 300pp.

LITTLEBURY BROS LTD.   Golf on Merseyside and district.
Second edition Liverpool. The authors, 1952. 48pp.

LOTHIAN REGIONAL COUNCIL. Department of Recreation and
Leisure   Golf: an interim strategy for provision in the
Lothian Region — a summary report.
Edinburgh, Lothian Regional Council, 1978.

McCUE, Carol   How to conduct golf club championships.
Evanston, Il, Golf Publishing Co., 1964. 16pp.

MACKENZIE, A.   Golf architecture: economy in course
construction and greenkeeping.
London, Simpkin, Marshall etc., 1920. 135pp.

McLEOD, Rod   St. Andrews Old, edited by Ken Thomson.
London, Souvenir Press, 1970. 128pp.

MADISON, John   Practical turfgrass management.
New York, Van Nostrand Reinhold, 1971. 466pp.

— Principles of turfgrass culture.
New York, Van Nostrand Reinhold, 1971. 420pp.

MALTBY, Ralph   Golf club design, fitting, alterations and
repair: the principles and procedures.
Newark, Oh, Faultless Sports, 1974. 331pp.

— Golf club repair in pictures.
Lake Park, Fl, Professional Golfers' Association of America
and Ralph Maltby Enterprises, 1978. 104pp.

MEW RESEARCH   The British golf market.
London, MEW, 1980. 8pp.

— The survey of British golfers.
London, MEW, 1979.

MILLER, Dick   America's greatest golfing resorts.
Indianapolis, Bobbs Merrill, 1977. 240pp.

MONDAY, Sil, *ed.*   Golf in the Ohio sun.
Cleveland, The author, 1970. 160pp.

MORRIS, John *and* COBB, Leonard   Great golf holes of Hawaii.
Auckland, NZ, Morris/Cobb Publications, 1977. 95pp.

— Great golf holes of New Zealand.
Auckland, NZ, Morris/Cobb Publications, 1971. 96pp.

MURRAY, C.M.   Greenkeeping in South Africa: a treatise on
scientific methods for the establishment and maintenance of
turf for sporting purposes and garden lawns.
Cape Town, South African Golf, 1932. 104pp.

MUSSER, H. Burton   Turf management.
New York, McGraw-Hill, 1962. 354pp.

MYERS, Kent C.   Golf in Oregon.
Portland, Oregon, Ryder Press, 1977. 154pp.

NATIONAL GOLF FOUNDATION   Availability of public
courses in US metropolitan areas.
North Palm Beach, Fl, The Foundation, 1977. 36pp.

— Golf course design: an introduction.
North Palm Beach, Fl, The Foundation, 197? 20pp.

159

— Golf driving range manual.
   North Palm Beach, Fl, The Foundation, 1978.

— Golf facilities in the United States.
   North Palm Beach, Fl, The Foundation, 1979. 12pp.
   Statistical report on the number of golfers in the United
   States on a state-by-state basis.

— Golf operations handbook.
   North Palm Beach, Fl, The Foundation, 1979. 468pp.

— Miniature putting course manual.
   North Palm Beach, Fl, The Foundation, 1978.

— Municipal golf course operational data, 1979.
   North Palm Beach, Fl, The Foundation, 1979.

— Organising and operating municipal golf courses.
   North Palm Beach, Fl, The Foundation. Annual publication.
   1979 edition. 466pp.

— The par-3 and executive golf course manual.
   North Palm Beach, Fl, The Foundation, 1977. 30pp.

— Planning and building the golf course.
   North Palm Beach, Fl, The Foundation, 1977. 30pp.

— Planning information for private and daily fee golf clubs.
   North Palm Beach, Fl, The Foundation, 1979. 480pp.

— Planning the golf clubhouse.
   North Palm Beach, Fl, The Foundation, 1977. 86pp.

— The professional golf shop.
   North Palm Beach, Fl, The Foundation, 1977. 96pp.

— Senior citizens and golf.
   North Palm Beach, Fl, The Foundation, 1979. 20pp.

NATIONAL PLAYING FIELDS ASSOCIATION   Sports
   ground maintenance: an elementary guide to club committees.
   London, The Association, 1978. 31pp.

— and SPORTS TURF RESEARCH INSTITUTE   Sports ground
construction: specifications.
London, The Association, 1975.

NEWMAN, Josiah   Newman's guide to London golf: being a
concise guide to the recognised golf clubs within 25 miles of
Charing Cross.
London, The Players Company, 1913. 288pp.

NORTHERN COUNCIL FOR SPORT AND RECREATION
Golf in the northern region.
Durham, The Council, 1978. 93pp. + appendices. This report
updates an earlier (1967) report. It examines the nature of
demand and supply of golf courses within the northern
region of England. It also attempts to estimate future
demand, investigates alternative provision strategies, and
makes recommendations about future provision, for local
authorities and the Regional Council. There are 100 courses
in the region.

PALMER, Arnold and BRUM, Bob   Arnold Palmer's best 54
holes.
New York, Doubleday, 1977. 206pp.

PENNINK, Frank   Frank Pennink's choice of golf courses.
London, A. and C. Black, 1976. 293pp. New York,
Transatlantic, 1977. Based on Frank Pennink's Golfer's
companion, q.v.

— Golf.
London, Garnett, 1952. 209pp. (Homes of sport series).
Thirty courses described and illustrated.

— Golfer's companion.
London, Cassell, 1962. 311pp.

PIPER, C.V. and OAKLEY, R.A.   Turf for golf courses.
New York, Macmillan, 1917. 262pp.

POLLARD, Frank C., *ed.*   Golf on the peninsula: an illustrated guide to the world famous golf courses on the Monterey peninsula.
Manhattan Beach, Ca, Course and Links Inc., 1973. 32pp.

PROFESSIONAL GOLFERS' ASSOCIATION OF AMERICA
Golf shop merchandising.
Lane Park, Fl, The Association, 197? 90pp.

— Golfer's atlas.
Lake Park, Fl, The Association, 197?.

SARAZEN, Gene *and* McLEAN, Peter   Golf: new horizons —
Pan Am's guide to golf courses around the world.
New York, Crowell, 1966. 276pp.

SCATCHED, Charles   Guide to Yorkshire golf.
Leeds, *Yorkshire Evening Post,* 1955. 79pp.

SCHARFF, Robert *and* editors of GOLF MAGAZINE, *eds.*
Great golf courses you can play: a guide to golf courses around the world.
New York, Scribners, 1974. 440pp.

SCOTT, Tom, *ed.*   AA guide to golf in Britain.
London, Octopus, 1977. 400pp. Comprehensive gazetteer to United Kingdom golf courses sponsored by the Automobile Association.

— Sixty miles of golf around London.
London, Barrie and Jenkins, 1975. 130pp. Previous edition entitled Fifty miles of golf around London. London, Jenkins, 1952. 184pp. Earlier editions of this title published by journal *Fairway and Hazard* in 1937, 1938 and 1939. The 1939 edition had 271pp.

SCOTTISH TOURIST BOARD   Scotland, home of golf.
Edinburgh, The Board, 1980. 41pp. Several earlier editions dating back to 1962 when it was entitled Scotland for golf.

SOMERSET SPORTS DEVELOPMENT COUNCIL   Golf:
a report prepared by the County Planning Officer for the
Somerset Sports Development Council.
Taunton, The Council 1969. 28pp.

SORENSON, Gary L.   The architecture of golf.
College Station, Texas, The author, 1976. 106pp. Includes a
useful bibliography on golf architecture.

SOUTH EASTERN MAGAZINES LTD.   Golfing in Kent:
a County Living handbook.
Maidstone, South Eastern Magazines Ltd., 1979. 36pp.
Guide to golf clubs in Kent, with a who's who of key figures
(golf club captains, secretaries etc.) and some fixtures for the
year.

SOUTH WESTERN SPORTS COUNCIL   Major recreation
survey Devon: golf courses 1971.
Exeter, Devon County Council, 1971. 31pp.

SPORTS COUNCIL   Provision for sport: indoor swimming
pools, indoor sports centres, golf courses.
London, Her Majesty's Stationery Office, 1972.

SPORTS COUNCIL FOR NORTHERN IRELAND   Existing
facilities — golf.
Belfast, The Council, 1978. 44pp.

SPORTS TURF RESEARCH INSTITUTE   Fertilizers in turf
culture.
Bingley, Yorks., The Institute, 1978.

— Turfgrass diseases.
Bingley, Yorks. The Institute, 1979.

— Turfgrass seed.
Bingley, Yorks. The Institute, 1980.

STEEL, Donald   The golf course guide to the British Isles.
Fifth edition. Glasgow, Collins for the *Daily Telegraph,*
1980. Several earlier editions starting in 1968.

STUART, Ian   Golf in Hertfordshire.
Hitchin, William Carling, 1972. 149pp.

STUTT, J. Hamilton   The reclamation of derelict lands for
golf.
London, Golf Development Council, 1980. 12pp.

SUTTON, Martin H.F., *ed.*   The book of the links: a symposium
on golf by Sir George Riddell, Bernard Darwin, Martin H.F.
Sutton, H.S. Colt, A.D. Hall, prize essay by a greenkeeper [and]
supplementary notes on manures, tables and miscellaneous
information.
London, W.H. Smith, 1912. 212pp.

— Lawns and sports grounds.
17th edition Reading, Sutton and Sons Ltd., 1962. 248pp.

— Layout and upkeep of golf courses and putting greens.
London, Simpkin Marshall, 1906. 42pp.

THOMAS, George C.   Golf architecture in America: its strategy
and construction.
Los Angeles, Times-Mirror Press, 1927. 342pp.

TOW, Kristin   International golf directory: resorts, clubs,
courses around the world.
Glendale, Ca, Ingledue and Associates, 1974. 112pp.

VEAL, A.J.   Sports and recreation in England and Wales.
Birmingham, Centre for Urban and Regional Studies,
University of Birmingham, 1977. (Research memorandum
74)

WAITE, Ken   A guide to golf in Lincolnshire.
Scunthorpe, Caldicotts, 197?. 34pp.

WARD-THOMAS, Pat   Shell golfer's atlas of England,
Scotland and Wales.
London, Joseph, 1968. 62pp.

— *and others*   The world atlas of golf.
London, Mitchell Beazley, 1976. 280pp. New York,
Random House, 1977. 280pp.

WELDON, Oliver J., *comp.*   Golfing in Ireland.
Dublin, General Publications Ltd., 1970. 142pp.

WENDEHACK, Clifford Charles   Golf and country clubs: a
survey of the requirements of planning, construction and
equipment of the modern club house.
New York, William Helburn, 1929. 51pp. + 157 plates.

WETHERED, H. Newton *and* SIMPSON, T.   The architectural
side of golf.
London, Longmans Green, 1929. 211pp. Revised edition
entitled Design for golf. London, Sportsmans Book Club,
1952. Classic book on golf architecture.

CHAPTER SIX

REFERENCE SOURCES AND THE PERIODICAL LITERATURE

All the material listed in this book is of some value as a source of reference, though much of it was not written with this purpose in mind. The items listed in this chapter, however, are *primarily* intended to answer specific queries, and in general their format and arrangement reflect this purpose. The categories defined for inclusion are encyclopaedias, compendia, directories (except those relating to golf courses, dealt with in the previous chapter), glossaries, dictionaries including biographical dictionaries, yearbooks and membership lists. Statistical reviews also figure prominently in the golfing literature as there is considerable fascination with records and with individual scores in major tournaments. The rules of golf are particularly complicated, and their definition and interpretation have also generated considerable documentation both by official bodies and by individual authors; this documentation is included in this chapter. Major bibliographies have also been identified and listed. Finally, brief reference is made to new non-literature-based sources such as computerised databases of bibliographic references and to information held in video-text systems such as British Telecom's Prestel service.

As far as can be determined, the first review article on golf to appear in a major general encyclopaedia was P.P. Alexander's contribution to volume 10 of the ninth edition of the *Encyclopaedia Britanica* published in 1879, though golf had been mentioned in this work as early as the third edition in 1797. Encyclopaedias devoted specifically to golf are a much more recent phenomenon, though some of the early general works often had an encyclopaedic quality about them even if not organised in such a precise way. Webster Evans' *Encyclopaedia of golf* (1971) claims to be the first A-Z work. Two more recent editions of this work have appeared, the latest in 1980; this has some 1,400 entries and copious cross-references. It also has an excellent and detailed index which makes it an invaluable quick reference guide. N.H. Gibson's *Encyclopaedia of golf* (1958) appeared somewhat earlier, and is basically a major statistical reference work, containing the "official all-time records". There was a revised second edition in 1964.

Others with the word "encyclopaedia" in their title include *Golf Magazine's encyclopaedia of golf* by John M. Ross and the editors of the journal. The third edition of this work has 439 pages and includes sections on history, major tournament and championship results, a golfing who's who, information on golf equipment, basic principles of the game, rules and etiquette, information on golf courses, and a glossary of terms. Another superb production which is packed with information on all aspects of the sport is the *Shell international encyclopaedia of golf* (1975) edited by Donald Steel and Peter Ryde. This book appeared in the United States under the simplified title *Encyclopaedia of golf.*

Other general reference texts with many of the characteristics of the all-embracing encyclopaedia include *The golfer's bible* by F.K. Allen and others. This is a wide-ranging reference tool with a special section within it devoted to women's golf. *The BBC book of golf*, edited by Ken Hawkes, is much briefer than some of the titles mentioned previously, and as well as emphasising the role of television in spreading the "gospel" of golf describes major tournaments and courses, and gives brief biographies of around 100 leading players. It includes a glossary of golf terms, and is well indexed. *America's golf book* published by *Golf Magazine* has a comprehensive records section, and covers the history of game, instruction and equipment, where to play, and how the game is governed. An unusual, and unstructured, collection of fascinating pieces of information about the game is George Houghton's *Believe it or not, that's golf* which contains "a miscellany of 1,000 oddities, facts and personal profiles". There is no doubt that many of these pieces of information are not recorded elsewhere, but the book would have been much more valuable as an information source had it been provided with an index. Other books, which might equally well have fitted into the anthologies chapter, include *The world of golf* (1970) by Dexter and McDonnell and *Golf: the passion and the challenge* (1977) by Mark Mulvoy and Art Spander. The latter is wide-ranging in its coverage of topics from golf course architecture to the modern professional golf tour, while Dexter's book is most useful for its biographical sketches of the players. Donald Steel's *Guinness book of golf facts and feats* (1980) is typical of the Guinness reference books, being produced to a high standard and possessing a very detailed index. *The whole golf catalog* (1980) by Larry Sheehan is also a valuable compendium by an expert in the field. It includes information on such topics as equipment manufacturers, tournament information, the major golfing organisations and the rules of golf.

As far as the British golfer is concerned, *The golfer's handbook*, which has appeared annually (with the exception of the war years) since 1898, is the prime source of current information and of the game's records. It has the same authority that Wisden's *Almanack* has for the cricketer. *The golfer's handbook* usually runs to some 700 pages, and includes records, organisations connected with the game, information on personalities, the rules, and very much more. It does not appear to circulate widely in the United States, and a selection of information from its pages was published in 1971 as a separate work for the American market by its then editor Percy Huggins. This was entitled *The golfer's miscellany*. Other important statistical handbooks on the game include the annual reference publication produced by the Professional Golfers' Association of America. The 1980 edition, entitled *The growth of golf*, also includes some more general articles.

Early yearbooks date back over a century, and one of the first was probably George Robb's *Manual of the Bruntsfield links*, which was a brief 16-page pamphlet first issued in 1868. Like many of its successors, this attempt at an annual publication soon fizzled out — the next year in fact. The historical link between cricket and golf, which has been noted elsewhere in this volume, shows up in *American cricket annual and golf guide*, which appeared from 1898 to 1901. It originated (surprisingly, considering the general apathy of most Americans towards the very English game of cricket) as a cricket annual, and added a golf section as the popularity of the game increased in the United States following the founding of the US Golf Association in 1896. Another early annual which was published for ten years from 1905 to 1914 was *Nisbet's golf year book*. This was originally edited by John L. Low, with later volumes being prepared by Vyvyan G. Harmsworth. This was a substantial directory of golf clubs which also included a who's who, information on the rules, and details of championships. The 1911 edition had 655 pages. *The golfing annual* had an even longer life span, lasting from 1888 to 1910; it included reviews of the year's championships and other material.

In the 1950s a number of short-lived annual reviews appeared. Leonard Crawley's *Playfair golf annual*, with statistics and summaries of events for the year, lasted five issues from 1950 to 1954. Others, such as John Barrington's *US golfers annual handbook*, failed to reach even a second issue.

The influence of, and interest in, the American professional golf tour began to generate statistical and other reference books on top professional golf. Harry Baron's *NBC sports golf guide, 1967* is a useful guide to professional golf in 1967, and includes information on leading players and courses, and statistics on the major championships. Mark McCormack's influence on the professional game has been considerable, and his companies have provided management services for some of the world's top players. *The world of professional golf* is a major annual reference work on the professional game, and details, in narrative and statistical formats, all the important happenings of the year under review. This annual started in 1967 as *Golf '67: world professional golf. Golf World* magazine (the American version of this title) has published *The world of golf* since 1973, while its British counterpart produced four annual volumes under the title *Piccadilly world of golf* between 1972 and 1975. The latter emphasised the European golf tour. The Professional Golfers' Association of America produces its annual *Official PGA tour media guide,* which includes tournament schedules, results from the previous year, and biographical information on tour participants.

In Britain, the Professional Golfers' Association (PGA) produces its own *Official tournament guide,* which is edited by public relations director George Simms. This has appeared annually since 1973. The Scottish region of the PGA produces *Scottish region tournament book,* and the Irish section published *Golf circuit,* a review of the past 12 months, which in 1977 was compiled and edited by Seamus Smith. Kenneth Roy's *Scottish golf directory* first appeared in 1980, and is scheduled as an annual yearbook and directory providing a comprehensive guide to both professional and amateur golf in Scotland.

Muir Maclaren produced at least three issues of *The Australian golfer's handbook* in 1957, 1960 and 1964, while *The DB golf annual* covered the golf tournament scene in both Australia and New Zealand for the years 1974-1977. Another authoritative annual edited by George Simms is *World of golf,* which appeared originally under the title of *The John Player golf yearbook* in its first issues. The sponsorship by major companies obviously provides considerable financial support in such a publishing enterprise where considerable costs are incurred in obtaining and cross-checking statistical and other information. Such sponsorship has its problems for the bibliographer. The changes which regularly occur as companies withdraw their support make it difficult sometimes to relate volumes to specific series.

The yearbooks published regularly, usually annually, by the golf unions are valuable sources of information on the amateur game especially in tracing names of officials and the dates and places for minor tournaments and matches. For club captains and other officials these documents are basic sources which are regularly referred to. *The golfing year* is the official yearbook of the English Golf Union, and during its lengthy existence it has been edited by some distinguished golf writers including Louis T. Stanley, whose output of golf books on all aspects of the game is formidable. *The lady golfers handbook* has been produced annually since 1894, and the current issue has over 200 pages of detailed information on all aspects of women's amateur golf in the United Kingdom and some overseas countries. Other similar works are the Scottish Golf Union's *Official yearbook* and the *English Ladies Golf Association Yearbook*. More periodical publications produced by these and similar bodies are discussed later in this chapter. Glossaries and dictionaries are often subsumed in other major works, as has been noted already, but some appear as separate volumes. One such is John Stobbs's *An ABC of golf* (1964) in which over 440 terms used in golf are defined and explained. Another is Hugh Taylor's *Golf dictionary* (1970) which includes terms and abbreviations in use in both America and Britain. Tom Scott's *Concise dictionary of golf* (1978) is a glossy production with more wide-ranging concerns including a substantial biographical section.

Biographical dictionaries have a considerable history, probably dating back to *Who's who in golf and directory of golf clubs and members* (1909) which provided approximately 1,000 pages of information at the amazing price of half a crown! (current equivalent 12½ pence). More recent biographical dictionaries include William Crehan's *Who's who in golf* (1971) and, with the same title, *Who's who in golf* (1976) by Len Elliott and Barbara Kelly. This latter volume includes brief biographies of some 400 players, administrators and others connected with the game.

171

The original documented rules of golf — 14 in all — were set out on one side of a sheet of paper. Today the rules are much more complex and, because of the vast sums of prize money available to the professional game, the understanding and interpretation of these rules has become crucial to all who play at the highest levels of the game. The arbiters of the rules are the Royal and Ancient Golf Club of St. Andrews in association with the United States Golf Association, and all official publications relating to rule changes emanate from these bodies. The rules, and decisions made in relation to them, are updated regularly, and in the case of the USGA *The rules of golf* is an annual publication. Since 1971 the same body has issued its *Decisions on the rules of golf* at similar intervals. The Royal and Ancient has similar procedures and, in addition to the basic written rule book, offers *Golf rules illustrated* which appears periodically with many illustrated examples. The fourth edition of this publication appeared following the most recent rules revision in January 1980. Joseph C. Dey, a former Executive Director of the USGA, also edits a similar American publication, *Golf rules in pictures,* which had reached its eighth edition by 1977. The wide availability of these official documents has not inhibited the generation of other publications on the rules of the game. One of the first was P.A. Vaile's *The illustrated rules of golf and the etiquette of the game* (1919). Other well-known writers and golfers have also made their contributions to this area of the literature. Robert Browning's *The golfer's catechism* (1935) and Francis Ouimet's *The rules of golf, illustrated and explained* (1948) are two conventional approaches, while Roger Hermanson's *Rules of golf in programmed form* (1968) introduced new teaching and communication ideas into a complicated field. Journalist and writer Peter Dobereiner revised his book on the rules, *Stroke, hole or match* (1976), to include the 1980 rule changes. The revision is titled, more basically, *Golf rules explained.* The leading American professional Tom Watson has made a special study of this topic and, in collaboration with Frank Hannigan, published his *Rules of golf illustrated and explained* in 1980. Problems of handicapping and of setting the standard scratch score for golf courses are of prime concern to amateur golfers and club officials. The Council of National Golf Unions, a body with representatives from all the national unions in the United Kingdom, is responsible in this sector. Their *Standard scratch score and handicapping scheme* had reached its sixth revised edition in 1975.

Bibliographical sources on the game of golf are in recent times dominated by Joseph Murdoch's indefatigable work. This draws considerably on pioneers such as Harry B. Wood, whose *Golfing curios and the like* (1910) contained an appendix comprising a bibliography of golf to that time. This book is primarily concerned with providing information on the implements of the game, on prints and engravings and all other forms of golfiana. There is also a brief history of the game. This book is highly valued by golf collectors, and was reprinted in facsimile by Pride Publications of Manchester in 1980. Another useful, though brief, contribution on the literature of the game appeared in Joyce Wethered *et al. The game of golf* (1931). This was a seven-page chapter by Horace H. Hutchinson who had produced a good deal of it up to that date! Another highly regarded definitive study is Cecil Hopkinson's *Collecting golf books* (1938) which was reprinted and expanded in 1980 with some additional material added by Joseph Murdoch. Murdoch himself produced a *tour-de-force* with his *Library of golf* (1968). This work covers material published between 1743 and 1966, and is a scholarly, but highly readable, source book with many annotated entries. It has excellent indexes by title, by subject matter, and by year of publication. Murdoch updated this work with a pamphlet, published in limited edition only, which covers the period 1966-1977 and corrects any errors subsequently found in the master work. Together with Janet Seagle, the librarian and curator of the United States Golf Association, Murdoch has also published *Golf: a guide to information sources* (1979). The first half of this book is devoted to annotated listings of selected important publications on golf arranged in various categories, while part two deals mainly with non-book information sources including audio-visual media, libraries, museums, booksellers, governing bodies and other institutions and agencies. It is a useful volume, though obviously biased strongly towards American sources. Murdoch is a founder member of the Golf Collector's Society and edits their bulletin. *The best of the Bulletin* (1978) includes selected items from issues published between 1970 (when it was established) and 1977. Typical of the type of material to be found here is a bibliography of song sheets relating to golf. A more specialised bibliography on greenkeeping in all its aspects is *Turfgrass bibliography from 1672 to 1972* (1977). This is a massive and authoritative work of over 700 pages compiled by James Beard and some colleagues.

The first journal devoted specifically to the game was *Golf,* which was sub-titled "A weekly record of ye royal and ancient game". This has continued to the present day as the current British weekly *Golf Illustrated* which is strongly oriented towards the local golf scene. It averages around 40 pages in each issue, and usually carries a good deal of job advertising for professionals, greenkeepers and club management personnel. Another early British journal, established as the weekly *Golfing and Cycling* in 1897, dropped its cycling interest after two years. It became a monthly, and was eventually absorbed into *Golf International* (1971-). The two most widely read British golf journals are *Golf Monthly* and *Golf World*, which both claim market leadership in the United Kingdom. Both have excellent contributors and provide good coverage of the game. Two more recently established journals of similar periodicity are *Par Golf*, established in 1974, and *Golf Scotland* (1980-) which, as its title implies, concentrates on golfing matters north of the border.

The world's leading golf journal is probably *Golf Digest*, a monthly published in Norwalk, Connecticut. It was established in 1950, and has developed a high reputation, especially for its instructional features. Another leading American journal is *Golf World*, a weekly based in Southern Pines, North Carolina, which places a special emphasis on tournament results. Other important American titles include *Sports Illustrated* which has a weekly circulation of over 2 million and which covers golf in addition to many other sports. *Golf* is a New York-based monthly, while *Senior Golfer*, which specialises in news and other information of particular relevance to older players, has been published in Florida since 1964.

The major organisations connected with golf produce periodicals and newsletters aimed at their members. *Professional Golf* and *Golf Trade Journal* are both official journals of the (British) Professional Golfers' Association. The former is a monthly restricted to members, while the latter appears ten times a year. The amateur game has similar dissemination media, and *Golf News and Fixtures*, which appears nine times a year, is produced by the English Golf Union. The *Scottish Golf Union Newsletter* (quarterly) serves a similar purpose for Scotland. This is a lively and well-produced journal which started publication in 1977.

The United States Golf Association produces its *Golf Journal* eight times a year, and the *PGA Magazine,* aimed at club professionals in particular, and published by their Association, appears monthly. This journal is also distributed to the media and to the golf equipment and apparel manufacturers. More locally-based American journals include *Northwest Golfer,* which is a monthly official publication of the Pacific Northwest Golf Association, and *Fore,* a quarterly produced by the Southern California Golf Association.

Some journals with a wider remit occasionally carry items of interest to some part of the golf world. *Sport and Leisure,* the official journal of the (British) Sports Council, is mainly devoted to wider sporting issues though it naturally reflects the Council's interests in the provision of facilities for all sporting activities, including golf. *Parks, Golf Course and Sports Grounds* is mainly of interest for the technical information on groundsmanship which it features. Other journals specifically aimed at the greenkeeper (or in American parlance, the golf course superintendent) include *Golf Greenkeeping and Course Maintenance,* published by the British Golf Greenkeeper's Association, *Golf Greenkeeper,* a commercially published journal issued ten times a year, and the Sports Turf Research Institute's *Sports Turf Bulletin.* The annual *Journal of the Sports Turf Research Institute* is an important, but rather specialised and advanced, technical work. The official journal of the Golf Course Superintendents Association of America, *The Golf Superintendent,* is mainly concerned with course maintenance, as is the *USGA Green Section Record* published six times a year by the United States Golf Association. *The International Greenkeeper* was established in 1970 by Donald Harradine, a leading golf course architect, to assist in improving the knowledge of greenkeepers on the continent of Europe. This journal appears three times a year in French/Spanish and German editions.

Trade journals of interest to the golf business include *Harpers Sports and Camping,* a fortnightly periodical covering all sport and leisure goods. It has occasional features on golf equipment. Other British journals include *Sports Trader,* a controlled-circulation journal distributed widely to sports goods retailers. An American trade magazine is *Golf Industry* based in Miami, Florida, and appearing monthly. *Golf Business* (Cleveland, Ohio) is aimed at club and course managements, and appears ten times per annum. In Britain, *Golf Club Management* claims to be the "only technical journal dealing with the problems of golf course and club house management, planning and design". It appears every two months, and is the official journal of the Association of Golf

175

Club Secretaries. *The Golf Club Steward and Caterer* also appears every two months, and 2,000 copies are distributed to golf clubs in England, Scotland and Wales.

As in all fields of interest, the periodical literature provides the most up-to-date information, and golf is no exception. Tracing particular articles is not easy, since many of the journals directly relevant to the industry are not indexed in secondary sources and do not appear in the major computerised databases now widely available. The Professional Golfer's Association of America has made a modest start (in 1979) to improve this situation. *Your reference guide to golf periodicals* appears twice a year, and indexes the articles appearing in eight leading golf journals. 26 subject headings are used. This guide is aimed at golf professionals who need to keep abreast of new developments in equipment and the like.

The databases of the United States National Technical Information Service (NTIS) and of Enviroline contain some technical references of relevance − mainly to report literature. A typical entry in these files is a report such as that produced by the Imperial College of Science and Technology, London on *Golf ball dynamics* (1975). The British Telecom viewdata system, Prestel, includes no fewer than nine golf files at the time of writing (January 1981). Most of the information contained is of general interest and includes files on golf courses by area, golf holidays and hotels in Europe and other overseas countries, golf fixtures in Europe for 1981, golfing records (based on the *Guinness book of golf facts and feats* listed in this chapter), information on golfing organisations and on the rules of the game and, for amusement, a golfing video game. Some of these files are very limited, especially the American Express file, which provides only a few golf club details for each main area of the United Kingdom. Undoubtedly this type of interactive file, which can reach individual homes and offices through the suitably converted television screen, has tremendous potential in such a sector where much of the information changes rapidly.

BIBLIOGRAPHY

REFERENCE WORKS

ALICOATE, John C., *ed.* Reference yearbook of golf.
Canoga Park, Ca, International Golfer, 1972. 992pp. Paperback edition 1973. 528pp. Attempts to list the names and
addresses of all golf clubs in North America. Also includes
golf equipment companies, biographies of leading players,
and much statistical material.

ALLEN, Frank Kenyon *and others* The golfer's bible.
New York, Doubleday, 1968. 159pp. Co-authors are Tom
LoPresti, Dale Mead and Barbara Romack. A wide-ranging
reference work.

ALLISON, Willie, *ed.* The first golf review.
London, Bonar Books, 1950. 92pp. Review of the previous
year's events; probably planned as an annual which did not
continue.

BARON, Harry, *ed.* NBC sports golf guide.
New York, Ridge Press and Grosset and Dunlap, 1967.
159pp.

BARRINGTON, John, *ed.* The US golfers annual handbook.
New York, Crowell, 1958. 248pp.

BARTLETT, Charles The new 1969 golfers almanac, edited by
Michael Bartlett.
New York, Bantam Books, 1969. 208pp. Excellent compila-
tion of facts and figures.

177

BEARD, James B., BEARD, Harriet J. *and* MARTIN, David P.
Turfgrass bibliography from 1672 to 1972.
East Lansing, Michigan, Michigan State University Press,
1977. 730pp. Major work of reference on all aspects of
growing grass. Covers the care and feeding of grass, diseases
and their cures and methods of building and maintaining
golf courses.

BRITISH GOLF UNIONS JOINT ADVISORY COUNCIL   The
standard scratch score and handicapping scheme . . . by the
Council of National Golf Unions.
Nottingham, The Council, 1975. 23pp.

BROWNING, Robert H.K.   The golfer's catechism: a vade
mecum to the rules of golf.
London, H.C. Quinn, 1935. 88pp.

CRAWLEY, Leonard, *ed.*   Playfair golf annual.
London, Playfair Books, Annual 1950-1954. Statistics and
summaries of events of the year under review.

CREHAN, William, *ed.*   Who's who in golf.
New York, Champion Sports Publishing, 1971. 130pp.

DEXTER, E.R. *and* McDONNELL, Michael, *eds.*   The world of
golf.
London, Purnell, 1970. 141pp. (World of sport library)

DEY, Joseph C.   Golf rules in pictures.
New York, Grosset and Dunlap, 1977. 96pp.

DOBEREINER, Peter   Golf rules explained.
Newton Abbot, David and Charles, 1980. 160pp. Previous
edition entitled Stroke, hole or match: golf rules explained.
1976. 192pp. United States edition entitled Golf explained:
how to take advantage of the rules. New York, Sterling
Publishing, 1977.

ELLIOTT, Len *and* KELLY, Barbara   Who's who in golf.
New York, Arlington House, 1976. 208pp.

ENGLISH GOLF UNION   The golfing year: the official hand
book of the English Golf Union.
Wokingham, Berks, The Union. Annual publication.

ENGLISH LADIES GOLF ASSOCIATION   Yearbook.
Otley, Yorks., The Association. Annual publication.

EVANS, Webster, *comp.*   Encyclopaedia of golf.
Third edition London, R. Hale, 1980. 320pp. Earlier
editions 1971 and 1974. Published in the United States, New
York, St. Martins Press.

FLANNERY, Jerome, *comp.*   American cricket annual and golf
guide.
New York, The author, 1898-1901.

GIBSON, Nevin Herman   The encyclopaedia of golf, with the
official all-time records.
Second edition New York, Barnes, 1964. 256pp. First
edition 1958. London, Kaye, 1959.

GOLF MAGAZINE   America's golf book.
New York, Scribners, 1970. 290pp.

GOLF WORLD MAGAZINE (London)   The Piccadilly world
of golf.
London, Wayland. Annual volume from 1972 to 1975.

GOLF WORLD MAGAZINE (Pinehurst)   The world of golf.
Southern Pines, NC, Golf World Inc. Annual volume 1973-.

GOLFER'S Handbook: world wide golf statistics, edited by
Eileen Gibb.
Glasgow, Golfers Handbooks. Annual, 1898-.

The GOLFING Annual.
London, Horace Cox. 1888 edition edited by C. Robertson
Bauchope, 1889 edition edited by John Bauchope, 1890-
1910 edited by David Scott Duncan.

GRAFFIS, Herb., *ed.*   Dictionary of golf information.
Chicago, Golfing Publications, 1960. 22pp.

HAWKES, Ken, *ed.*   BBC book of golf.
London, British Broadcasting Corporation, 1975. 144pp.

HERMANSON, Roger H.   The rules of golf in programmed form.
West Palm Beach, Fl, Professional Golfers Association of America, 1968. 118pp.

HOPKINSON, Cecil   Collecting golf books, 1743-1938: to which has been added *Bibliotheca Golfiana* together with some notes and commentary by Joseph S.F. Murdoch.
Droitwich, Grant Books, 1980. 90pp. Original edition (without the contribution from Murdoch) London, Constable, 1938. 56pp. (Aspects of book collecting series)

HOUGHTON, George   Believe it or not, that's golf: a miscellany of 1,000 oddities, facts and personal profiles.
London, Luscombe, 1974. 199pp. New York, Hippocrene Books, 1975.

HUGGINS, Percy, *ed.*   The golfer's miscellany.
New York, Harper and Row, 1971. 176pp. Selection of information contained in The Golfer's handbook which Huggins then edited.

LADIES GOLF UNION   The lady golfer's handbook.
St. Andrews, The Union. Annual volume 1894-.

LOW, John L., *ed.*   Nisbet's golf year book.
London, James Nisbet. Annual 1905-1914. Later editions edited by Vyvyan G. Harmsworth.

McCORMACK, Mark H., *ed.*   Dunhill golf year book.
London, Springwood Books, 1980. 447pp. Contains brief reports on all major professional tournaments and the previous year's statistical record.

— The world of professional golf: Mark H. McCormack's golf annual.
Annual, 1967-. Originally published as Golf '67: world professional golf. London, Cassell, 1967. Subsequent editions published in Britain by Hodder and Stoughton, 1968-1971,

Collins, 1972-1977, and Angus and Robertson, 1978-.
United States editions published New York, Atheneum
Press.

MACLAREN, Muir   The Australian golfer's handbook, 1957.
Sydney, Langside Publishing, 1957. 256pp. Later editions
in 1960 and 1964.

McLEAN, T.P. *and* WALLACE, A.J.   The DB golf annual.
Auckland, NZ, Moa Publications. Annual 1974-1977.

MULVOY, Mark *and* SPANDER, Art   Golf: the passion and
the challenge.
Englewood Cliffs, NJ, Prentice-Hall, 1977. 256pp. Covers a
wide range of topics from course architecture through
equipment, to the modern professional tour. Well produced
with many excellent photographs.

MURDOCH, Joseph S.F.   The best of the Bulletin: a selection
of "scraps and patches" from the Golf Collector's Society
Bulletin, 1970-1977.
Lafayette Hill, Pa, Golf Collectors Society, 1978. 60pp.

— The library of golf (1743-1966): a bibliography of books,
indexed alphabetically, chronologically and by subject matter.
Detroit, Gale Research Company, 1968. 314pp.

— The library of golf 1743-1966 revised, 1967-1977 added.
Lafayette Hill, Pa, The author, 1978. 56pp.

— *and* SEAGLE, Janet   Golf: a guide to information sources.
Detroit, Gale Research Company, 1979. 232pp. (Sports,
games and pastimes information guide series, no. 7).

OUIMET, Francis   The rules of golf (revised), illustrated and
explained.
New York, Garden City Publishing, 1948. 90pp.

PIGNON, F.J.C., *ed.*   Spalding golfer's year book 1960.
London, S. Paul, 1960. 127pp.

PROFESSIONAL GOLFERS' ASSOCIATION   The Professional Golfers' Association 1980 Yearbook.
     Sutton Coldfield, The Association, 1980. 160pp. Distributed free to all members of the Association. The first to be issued for ten years.

— Irish Section   Golf circuit: a review of the past twelve months.
     1977 edition compiled and edited by Seamus Smith. Dublin, Tara Publishing. 68pp. Annual publication.

— Scottish Region   PGA Scottish region tournament book.
     Newburgh, The Association, 1977. 99pp. Cover title: Golf Scotland 77.

PROFESSIONAL GOLFERS' ASSOCIATION OF AMERICA The growth of golf: 1980 book of golf.
     Lake Park, Fl, The Association. Annual publication.

— Official PGA tour media guide.
     Lake Park, Fl, The Association. Annual publication.

— Your reference guide to golf periodicals.
     Lake Park, Fl, The Association. 1979-. Two issues per annum.

PUCKETT, Earl and CROMIE, Bob, eds. Golfer's digest.
     Seventh edition. Chicago, Follett, 1976.

RAND McNALLY   All about golf.
     Chicago, Rand McNally, 1975. 195pp.

RICHARDSON, Donald H., ed. World wide golf directory.
     Washington, DC, World Sports, 1973. 160pp. Second edition entitled Gene Sarazen's world golf directory, edited by Joseph Gambatese, 1977.

ROBB, George, comp.   Manual of the Bruntsfield links.
     Edinburgh, Allied Club, 1867. 16pp. There was also an 1868 edition.

ROSS, John M. *and* editors of GOLF MAGAZINE, *eds.*
Golf Magazine's encyclopaedia of golf. Third edition updated
and revised, New York, Harper and Row, 1979. 439pp.
Previous editions 1970 and 1973, edited by Robert Scharff
and the editors of *Golf Magazine*

ROY, Kenneth, *ed.*   Scottish golf directory: a comprehensive
guide to golf in Scotland, professional and amateur.
Maybole, Ayrshire, Kenneth Roy Publishers, 1980.

ROYAL AND ANCIENT GOLF CLUB OF ST. ANDREWS
Golf rules illustrated: an official publication of the Royal
and Ancient Golf Club of St. Andrews.
Fourth edition Glasgow, Munro-Barr Publications, 1980.
Includes complete rules as revised up to January 1980,
with many illustrated examples and interpretations.

— The rules of golf
St Andrews, Royal and Ancient Golf Club, 1980.

SCOTT, Tom   The concise dictionary of golf.
London, Bison Books, 1978. 256pp.

— *and* EVANS, Webster, *eds.*   The golfer's year.
London, Kaye, 1950. London Sportsmans Book Club,
1951. 2 volumes. Volume 1 reviews aspects of the previous
year's golf. Volume 2 is an anthology of essays on the game.

SCOTTISH GOLF UNION   Official yearbook.
Edinburgh, The Union. Annual publication.

SHEEHAN, Larry, *ed.*   The whole golf catalog.
New York, Atheneum Press, 1980. 292pp.

SIMMS, George, *ed.*   The official tournament guide.
London, Professional Golfers' Association. Annual, 1973—.

— The world of golf.
London, Queen Anne Press. Annual from 1977 under current
title. 1973-1976 appeared as John Player golf yearbook
edited by Ken Schofield.

STEEL, Donald   The Guinness book of golf facts and feats.
London, Guinness Superlatives, 1980. 256pp.

— *and* RYDE, Peter, *eds.*   Shell international encyclopaedia of
golf.
London, Pelham, 1975. 480pp. United States edition
entitled Encyclopedia of golf. New York, Viking Press,
1975.

STOBBS, John   An ABC of golf.
London, S. Paul, 1964. 252pp.

TAYLOR, Hugh, *ed.*   Golf dictionary.
London, F.C. Avis, 1970. 240pp.

The TOURNAMENT player: golf annual 1978.
San Diego, Ca, Scott-Stuart Sports Inc. Annual?
Includes statistics, tour schedules and biographies.

TYLER, Martin, *ed.*   The sportsman's world of golf.
London, Marshall Cavendish, 1976. 152pp. Some of the
material in this publication appeared originally in part-
works.

UNITED STATES GOLF ASSOCIATION   Decisions on the
rules of golf.
Far Hills, NJ, The Association. Annual. 1971-.

— The rules of golf.
Far Hills, NJ, The Association. Annual publication.

VAILE, P.A.   The illustrated rules of golf and the etiquette
of the game.
Chicago, T.E. Wilson, 1919. 84pp.

WATSON, Tom *and* HANNIGAN, Frank   The rules of golf
illustrated and explained.
New York, Random House, 1980. 200pp.

WHO'S who in golf and directory of golf clubs and members.
London, Stanley Publishing, 1909. *c*.1,000pp.

WOOD, Harry B.   Golfing curios and "the like": with an
    appendix comprising a bibliography of golf etc.
    London, Sherratt and Hughes, 1910. 149pp. Facsimile
    reprint Manchester, Pride Publications, 1980.

SELECTED GOLF PERIODICALS

AUSTRALIAN GOLF   Sydney, Australia.
    Monthly.

COUNTRY CLUB GOLFER   Irvine, Ca
    Monthly 1971-.

FSGA GOLF NEWS   Sarasota, Fl.
    Monthly.

FLORIDA GOLFWEEK   Winter Haven, Fl.
    Weekly.

FORE   North Hollywood, Ca.
    Quarterly. Official publication of the Southern California
    Golf Association.

GOLF   New York, NY.
    Monthly.

GOLF BUSINESS   Cleveland, Oh.
    Ten issues per year.

GOLF CLUB MANAGEMENT: official journal of the
    Association of Golf Club Secretaries. London.
    Bi-monthly. 1942-.

GOLF CLUB STEWARD AND CATERER: official journal
    of the Golf Club Stewards Association (incorporates *19th Hole*)
    Watford, Herts.
    Bi-monthly.

GOLF COLLECTORS' SOCIETY BULLETIN   Lafayette Hill, Pa.
   Irregular? No. 1 1970-.

GOLF DIGEST   Norwalk, Ct.
   Monthly. 1950-.

GOLF FORUM   Sepulveda, Ca.
   Monthly. Official publication of the Southern California Public Links Golf Association.

GOLF GREENKEEPER   London.
   Ten issues per year.

GOLF GREENKEEPING AND COURSE MAINTENANCE
   Official journal of the British Golf Greenkeepers Association.

GOLF ILLUSTRATED   London.
   Weekly. 1890-. From 1890-1899 published under the title Golf: a weekly record of ye Royal and Ancient game.

GOLF IN AUSTRALIA   Surrey Hills, NSW.
   Monthly.

GOLF INDUSTRY   North Miami, Fl.
   Monthly. Trade journal.

GOLF INTERNATIONAL   London.
   Fortnightly. 1971-. Superseded Golf Weekly.

GOLF JOURNAL   Far Hills, NJ.
   Eight issues per year. Official journal of the United States Golf Association.

GOLF MARKET REPORT   North Palm Beach, Fl.
   Monthly.

GOLF MONTHLY   Glasgow.
   Monthly. 1911-.

GOLF NEWS AND FIXTURES: official journal of the English
Golf Union. Wokingham, Berks.
Nine issues per year.

GOLF SCOTLAND   Glasgow.
Monthly. 1980-.

GOLF SHOP OPERATIONS   Norwalk, Ct. 1962-.
(formerly Pro shop operations).

THE GOLF SUPERINTENDENT   Lawrence, Kansas.
Ten issues per year. 1926-. Official journal of the Golf
Course Superintendents of America. Formerly Golf Course
Reporter.

GOLF TRADE JOURNAL: official magazine of the
Professional Golfers' Association.
Ten issues per year. 1969 — (incorporates *Golfing Magazine*).

GOLF WORLD   London.
Monthly. 1970-.

GOLF WORLD   Southern Pines, NC.
Weekly.

GOLFER   Cleveland, Ohio.
Monthly. Newspaper aimed at amateur golfers and country
clubs in the Cleveland area.

GOLFER   Johannesburg, SA Journal of the Transvaal
Provincial Golf Association (in Afrikaans and English).

GOLFER'S COMPANION   Dublin.
Three times per year. 1974-.

GOLFORUM   North Palm Beach, Fl.
Quarterly.

GROUNDSMAN: official journal of the Institute of
Groundsmanship. London.
Monthly. 1934-.

HARPERS SPORTS AND CAMPING   London.
    Fortnightly. 1930-.

INTERNATIONAL GREENKEEPER   Caslano, Switzerland.
    Three issues per year. 1970-. Two editions appear in French/
    Spanish and German.

LADIES GOLF   St Andrews.
    Eight issues per year.

MGA NEWSLETTER   New York, NY.

METROPOLITAN PGA INC. NEWSLETTER   New Rochelle,
    NY.
    Monthly.

MINNESOTA GOLFER   Minneapolis, Minn
    Quarterly.

MUNICIPAL GOLF COURSES NEWSLETTER   Los Angeles
    Ca.
    Monthly. Produced by Los Angeles City Recreation and
    Parks Department.

NATIONAL CLUB ASSOCIATION NEWSLETTER
    Washington, DC.
    Monthly.

NEW ZEALAND GOLF NEWS   Auckland, NZ.
    Monthly.

NORTHWEST GOLFER   Bellevue, Washington.
    Monthly. Official publication of the Pacific Northwest Golf
    Association.

PGA MAGAZINE   Lake Park, Fl.
    Monthly. Official publication of the Professional Golfers'
    Association of America.

PGA TOUR NEWS   Washington, DC.
    Monthly.

PAR GOLF   London.
   Monthly. 1974-.

PARKS, GOLF COURSES AND SPORTS GROUNDS   London.
   Monthly.

PIN-HIGH: a magazine for women golfers
   Darlington, 1966-?

POPULAR GOLF   London.
   1954-?

PROFESSIONAL GOLF: official journal of the Professional
   Golfers' Association, Sutton Coldfield
   Monthly. 1920-.

RECREATION MANAGEMENT   Leigh-on-sea, Essex.
   Monthly.

SCOTTISH GOLF UNION NEWSLETTER.   Edinburgh.
   Quarterly. 1977-.

SENIOR GOLFER   Clearwater, Fl.
   Quarterly. 1964-.

SOUTH AFRICAN GOLF   Johannesburg, SA
   Monthly.

SOUTH AUSTRALIAN GOLFER   Port Adelaide, South
   Australia.
   Monthly.

SOUTHERN GOLF   Elm Grove.
   Quarterly. 1969-. (formerly Southern Golf Course
   Operations.)

SPORT AND LEISURE: official journal of the Sports Council
   (includes Sports Development Bulletin Supplement).
   Bi-monthly. 1949-. Originally titled Physical Recreation.

SPORTS AND GAMES DEALER   London.
   Monthly.

SPORTS ILLUSTRATED   New York. NY.
    Weekly. 1954-.

SPORTS TRADE NEWS   London.
    Monthly.

SPORTS TRADER: the British journal of sports goods and
    equipment. London.
       Fortnightly. 1907-.

SPORTS TURF BULLETIN   Bingley, Yorks.
    Quarterly.

SPORTS TURF RESEARCH INSTITUTE JOURNAL   Bingley,
    Yorks.
       Annual.

USGA GREEN SECTION RECORD   Far Hills, NJ.
    Six issues per year. Official agronomy publication of the
    United States Golf Association.

USGA NEWSLETTER   Far Hills, NJ.
    Three issues per year. Sent to member clubs.

CHAPTER SEVEN

GOLFING
ORGANISATIONS

The organisational sources of information on the game of golf are many and diverse. *The golfer's handbook* lists over 260 world-wide, although many of these are relatively small and run by voluntary staff. Their ability to deal with requests for informa-tion is therefore entirely dependent on the available time and goodwill of those responsible. In consulting many in the prepara-tion of this sourcebook it has been found that many *are* extremely knowledgeable and often willing to help insofar as they can.

Before considering individual bodies and their information potential it may be useful to indicate briefly the structure of this chapter. Firstly, some of the organisations dealing with general aspects of sport provision and recreation management are con-sidered. The game's governing bodies and the organisations which further the interests of both the amateur and professional game come next. The various aspects of the golf business such as golf course architects, greenkeepers and club secretaries follow.

Finally, reference is made to some of the more important publicly-available libraries and museums which have relevant material. Private collectors have a considerable amount of infor-mation in their possession but since access to this material is limited they are not listed.

Within the United Kingdom, general oversight of sports manage-ment is exercised by the Minister responsible for sport, who is a junior minister within the Department of the Environment. The Sports Council, with its regionally-based satellite bodies, provides the main instrument for overall sports planning, and especially for the provision of the appropriate facilities. Much of this provi-sion is by private enterprise, and this is the case with the majority of golf clubs and other facilities, but financial and other assistance is made available through the regional sports councils to a limited extent. The Sports Council is based in London, and has an Information Centre with a substantial collection of books, reports, journals and other documents. This collection is accessible to *bona fide* enquirers during normal office hours. Most of the material collected is on general sports planning and provision, and individual sports are only represented to a limited extent. Nevertheless the Information Centre does contain some important material and is of considerable value to those requiring information on provision of facilities. The Council's regional organisations usually publish annual reports which include data on their activities. In some cases the regional councils have their own information and library facilities. For example, the East Midlands Sports Council based in Nottingham has an information unit containing over 2,500 documents, 65 current periodicals and audiovisual and trade materials. This Council also publishes an occasional *Information Bulletin* aimed at local authorities and other agencies within the region. Several of the Regional Councils have published reports on golf provision in their regions, and these are valuable sources of (fairly current) information. The Northern Council produced *Golf in the Northern Region* (1978), a 93-page separate document (listed in Chapter 5), while others, such as the Eastern Region Sports Council, have included information on golf within more general reports on sports provision. Others have sponsored and organised symposia and conferences on golf course provision. These include the Greater London and South East Sports Council who published the papers of such a conference in the *Provision, finance and management of golf facilities for public use* (1973), and the Eastern Region Sports Council who held a conference on an identical topic in the same year in collaboration with the Golf Development Council (GDC). The Scottish Sports Council also collaborated with the GDC in 1976 on *The teaching of golf in schools,* the papers of which have also been published. The Sports Council for Wales has a number of publications available, many of them free of charge. Most are on general sports provision, though one — *Golf courses in Wales* — is specifically relevant. The Sports Council for Northern Ireland provides advisory services to the provincial government (at the time of writing the Northern Ireland Office) and the local authorities. It published an inventory of golf provision in the province under the title *Existing facilities — golf* (1978) which supplemented some earlier data collection studies carried out in 1971.

The Sports Council jointly sponsored the Sports Documentation Centre located within the University of Birmingham Library until 1980. This sponsorship has now been withdrawn, and the Centre is currently resourced totally by the University. Its primary function is to serve the university's Physical Education Department, but it is still accessible to all individuals and organisations involved in serious research into sport, physical education and recreation. Its subject coverage, though diverse, leans towards the more scientific aspects of the field, including material on comparative studies and the psychology, sociology and philosophy of physical activity, in addition to information on sports medicine and biomechanics. For those interested in golf it is of limited value, though because of its comprehensive bibliographic collection it is important as a resource for more academic literature searches. Its collection includes over 2,000 books, pamphlets, conference proceedings, reports, theses and government publications, and a collection of over 400 bibliographies. It publishes the *Sports Documentation Monthly Bulletin* which lists relevant articles from the 175 journals taken by the Centre and from conference papers. This has appeared regularly since 1971. The Centre offers an enquiry service, and lists of references are supplied with photocopies of original articles subject to the provisions of the British Copyright Act 1956. Recent reading lists compiled by the Centre on golf topics include *The biomechanics of the golf swing* and *Some aspects of golf and golf course management*.

The Library of the Departments of the Environment and Transport can also be considered as a basic general resource for sports information. It is accessible to *bona fide* users by appointment, and its document input is selectively listed in the fortnightly *Library Bulletin* which is available on subscription from the Department in Marsham Street, London. Relatively little information specific to golf is included, though many of the local authority structure plans and other supporting documents which are collected by the library include relevant information on sports provision. Some of the local authorities themselves (through their planning departments) hold considerable data of relevance to golf course provision in their areas, and some of this is published, usually in more general topic reports on recreation and leisure. The more important local authority libraries, such as the Greater London Council Research Library, hold relevant material from their own and other authorities. The GLC material is publicly accessible through the monthly abstract journal *Urban Abstracts* and through the ACOMPLIS data base, which includes some 80,000 items on all aspects of urban management. This database is now publicly available on-line through the European Space Agency Recon system.

Other organisations with wide-ranging interests in the recreation management field include the Institute of Park and Recreation Administration which publishes the *Journal of Parks and Recreation* and has its own library. It has no publications specifically on golf. The Institute of Recreation Management is another relevant professional body and publishes the irregular *Recreation management directory* which includes many useful addresses. The Leisure Studies Association is a small organisation bringing together academics and practitioners in all sectors of leisure and recreation provision. It has a membership of some 300 individuals. It has no publications of direct relevance to the game of golf but is useful for contacts in the research field. An American organisation, the Washington-based National Recreation and Parks Association, publishes a valuable *Bibliography of theses and dissertations in recreation, parks, camping and outdoor education* (1970) which is also useful mainly to academic researchers. The Association's management aids series includes Cook and Holland's *Public golf courses* (1964) (listed in Chapter 5) and a pamphlet on *Par-3 golf.*

The general recreation management organisations and governmental bodies are diverse and numerous, and it is possible only to give an indication of the range of sources of information available in this wider context.

Specifically relevant to golf are organisations which act as advisory bodies, as is the case with the Golf Development Council (GDC). The GDC advises the Sports Council and its Regional Councils on all planning and design aspects of golf provision. It was founded in 1965 and, in addition to providing direct advice, also arranges conferences, study sessions and training courses. Its publications include *Elements of golf course layout and design* (listed in Chapter 5), *Golf clubhouses: a planning guide* and *Analyses of current costs.* The Golf Foundation has a somewhat related function, especially in its training aspects, and provides support, training and general encouragement for younger players to take up the game. It is a non-profit-making body financed mainly by the golf equipment firms and by profits from competitions organised by professional golfers. The Golf Foundation is particularly influential in the schools. It publishes an annual report

194

and occasional publications on particular topics within its fields of interest.

The ruling authority for the game is the Royal and Ancient Golf Club of St. Andrews which was founded in 1754. The R and A is still a private club with an individual membership of some 1,750 individuals. Through its Committees on the Rules of Golf Implements and Balls, and Amateur Status, it controls the development of the game in association with the United States Golf Association. The R and A also organises the Open Championship and other international tournaments. It has an excellent museum containing many early golf clubs, balls and other implements associated with the game, as well as its precious collection of club trophies. Its library contains some 1,500 volumes plus bound sets of important golf periodicals. It is expected that the library will be re-organised and may be made more accessible to non-members of the club. At the present time, those wishing to visit the museum and use the library need to make prior arrangements with the Secretary of the Club.

The United States Golf Association (USGA) was founded in 1894, and its activities include rule making and decisions on the rules, maintaining the system of handicapping, testing of new equipment, and defining amateur status. It is also involved, through the USGA Green Section, in assisting member clubs in maintenance and upkeep of golf courses, and provides a turfgrass advisory service and sponsors turf research. It established its library and museum in 1936, and the collections are available to the public. The library is probably the most comprehensive in existence, and in 1974 had some 6,000 volumes. The USGA has a major publications programme on the rules of golf, handicapping and course rating, golf course maintenance, and on particular topics such as safety on the golf course and aspects of equipment. It publishes *The Golf Journal* eight times a year and the *USGA Green Section Record* every two months. In 1974 it issued *A brief introduction to the museum and library of the United States Golf Association* which gives basic historical information on the Association and describes the resources and collections held by the library and museum.

The professional game has its own administrative structure on both sides of the Atlantic. In Britain, the Professional Golfers' Association (PGA) is the governing body of the professional game, and serves the needs of both the club and the tournament-playing professional. Within the framework of the PGA is the European

Tournament Players' Division which is responsible for organisation and administration of tournaments. The PGA publishes a *Yearbook* and a monthly magazine *Professional Golf (see* also Chapter 5) which is restricted to members only. The annual report of the Association is also made available to members. The 1980 *Yearbook* includes general articles on the game, a list of members and byelaws, procedures and rules and regulations of the Association. The Women's Professional Golf Association was founded in 1979 and governs the emerging WPGA tournament circuit in the United Kingdom.

There are American equivalents to these organisations, and the Professional Golfers' Association of America (USPGA), founded in 1916, claims to be the largest working sports organisation in the world. According to its 1979 Annual Report, it has a membership of around 8,300 full members, most of whom are club professionals, plus almost 4,000 apprentices under training. The USPGA has 40 geographically-based sections covering the whole of the United States. It has an impressive list of publications on all aspects of the game, and also provides films, slides, cassette tapes and other materials to its members and for general use. The Association conducts championships and provides guidelines for members' conduct and duties as well as operating educational programmes. As in Britain, the organisation of the tournament circuit, or "the tour" as it is known, is handled by a separate division. This is the PGA Tour based, like the parent organisation, in Florida. The women's professional game is controlled by the Ladies' Professional Golf Association (LPGA), based in New York and established in 1950. The International Golf Association, also based in New York, is responsible for the annual professional World Cup event in which two players from each competing country take part. This event is of great value to those countries whose players are not of the standard to compete in the United States tour and the other major circuits in Europe and the Far East.

Although the professional game is often seen as the "shop window" of golf because of the large amounts of prize money at stake and the increasing coverage by the communications media, it is the amateur game which provides the grass roots of the game. In Britain the national golf unions further the interests of the game at club level and administer international and domestic competitions. The Scottish Golf Union is the governing body for the amateur game in Scotland and has a membership of around 150,000 individual members and 620 affiliated clubs. It publishes an official yearbook and a quarterly *Newsletter*. The Welsh Golfing Union is much smaller, though it is some 25 years older than the Scottish Union. It is organised into eight districts and has a membership of 108 clubs and societies. The Welsh Union publishes an annual report. The objectives of the English Golf Union, founded in 1924, are to further the interests of the amateur game in England, to assist in maintaining a uniform system for handicapping, and to arrange amateur championships. Its annual publication, *The golfing year*, is a substantial information source containing statistics, names and addresses of officials, and similar material. It also publishes a journal, *Golf News and Fixtures*, nine times a year. Co-ordination of the national unions is organised through the Council of National Golf Unions which consists of representatives from the Unions mentioned, together with the Golfing Union of Ireland which has similar functions and responsibilities. The European Golf Association links the national amateur golf unions of 20 European countries. It is based in Paris. It co-ordinates the dates of national championships, and arranges international matches. It was founded in 1937 and its 16-page *Constitution* is published in both English and French.

The women's amateur game in Britain is governed by the Ladies' Golf Union (LGU) based in St. Andrews. It has a membership of some 145,000 individual players, 1,750 British organisations and 2,500 overseas bodies. The national golf associations of England and Scotland and the Irish and Welsh Unions are part of this membership, and the LGU exercises a comprehensive control of all aspects of the women's game. It publishes an annual *Lady golfer's handbook* and a journal, *Ladies Golf*, which appear eight times each year. The English Ladies' Golf Association (ELGA) also publishes a yearbook which contains a list of affiliated clubs with the number of women members and the standard scratch score for each course. The ELGA member clubs are issued with an annual report and statement of accounts. The Scottish Ladies' Golfing Association (SLGA) has a membership of 328 clubs, and promotes all aspects of women's golf in Scotland. It produces no publications except for its annual report, which is not generally available. The SLGA is also based at St. Andrews. A *History of the Scottish Ladies Golfing Association: 1903-1928* was published in London, and covers its earlier years.

The Golf Foundation (of Britain) has already been mentioned. Its backing comes from the golf business, and its overall aims are to increase the game's popularity, especially by encouraging junior players. The American National Golf Foundation (NGF) has similar objectives but is a very much more powerful and influential body than its British counterpart. The NGF is backed by the golf equipment makers and other golf-related industries. It was originally based in Chicago from its foundation in 1936, but in the 1970s it relocated in North Palm Beach, Florida. It claims to be "the nation's clearing house of golf information" and produces many publications on golf course planning and operation as well as instructional material in both documentary and audio-visual formats. Serial publications include *Golf Market Report*, a monthly aimed at golf-oriented businesses, and *Golf-orum*, a quarterly newsletter aimed at golf clubs and courses. Many of the NGF's excellent manuals and statistical publications have been listed in previous chapters of this work. Another recently formed body based in the United States is the International Association of Golf Administrators, which is primarily an information exchange organisation with some 40 members from state and national golf associations. It was founded in 1969 as the complexities of managing all the strands of the game were becoming increasingly obvious.

Designers and builders of golf courses and facilities have their own trade associations. The British Association of Golf Course Architects is a small group of ten firms, while the American Society of Golf Course Architects has a membership of 75 including some in Canada and Mexico. The British Association published its *Rules* in 1972, and from 1980 has produced an *Information Bulletin* twice a year. The American body is more prolific in its dissemination of information, and issues various leaflets including *Selecting your golf course architect, Planning the real estate development golf course, Planning the municipal golf course* and *Master planning — the vital first steps in golf course construction*. It also issues a regularly up-dated *Membership list* and *Guide to professional practice under the code of ethics*. The Golf Course Builders of America, Inc has no direct counterpart in Britain. It brings together those involved in building and equipping new courses, remodelling existing courses, developing irrigation projects and the like. It has a membership of 31 companies, and publishes its own *Yearbook and directory*. The work of the United States Golf Association Green Section has already been referred to. In Britain many of the services offered by this body are provided by the Sports Turf Research Institute based at Bingley in West Yorkshire. This Institute is a non-profit-making body providing

198

advice, education and research and, although it serves the interests of other sports organisations interested in turf management, the golf sector was prime motivating force behind its foundation in 1930. This involvement has been maintained, and there are close links between the Institute and the four national golf unions. In addition a substantial number of individual golf clubs are members. The Institute publishes its *Sports Turf Bulletin* quarterly, and its weighty and authoritative *Journal* appears once a year.

Organisations bringing together greenkeepers (or the American golf course superintendents) include the British Golf Greenkeepers' Association, which was established in 1920 and publishes the *British Golf Greenkeeper* on a monthly basis. The International Greenkeepers' Association was founded in 1970 (as was mentioned earlier) by golf architect Donald Harradine with the objective of improving the knowledge of greenkeepers on the continent of Europe who are not familiar with the English language. It holds seminars in French, German and Spanish, and its newsletter *The International Greenkeeper* is published in those languages. The Golf Course Superintendents' Association of America was founded in 1927 and by 1980 had a membership of over 3,200. It collects and disseminates technical information on golf course management for the benefit of its members through a publications programme which includes a monthly magazine and a quarterly newsletter.

Golf club management is the concern of the Association of Golf Club Secretaries which was founded in 1933 and has a membership of some 1,200 who work for private golf clubs. Most members are with British golf clubs, but some are from overseas countries. The Association publishes a *List of members*, its *Rules* and a bi-monthly magazine *Golf Club Management*. The Golf Club Stewards' Association represents the interests of catering staff in golf clubs, and produces the bi-monthly journal *Golf Club Steward and Caterer*. The Club Managers' Association of America has around 3,000 members, of whom about half are managers of private golf clubs. The Association has a substantial publications programme on many aspects of club management, not all of which are specific to golf. One which is relevant is *Golf courses: a guide to analysis and valuation* (1980) which was produced by the American Institute of Real Estate Appraisers. Many of the publications issued are on accounting, club management and catering.

The National Golf Clubs' Advisory Association, based in Richmond, Surrey, provides advice, particularly on legal issues, to its membership of some 850 golf clubs. The Association publishes a yearbook and was established in 1922. An American organisation with somewhat similar functions is the National Club Association. It has the characteristics of a trade association and lobbying group, maintaining contact with United States government agencies on matters such as tax and personal issues. It communicates data collected through a publications programme, through seminars, and through the individual counselling of golf clubs. The National Association of Public Golf Courses is primarily to unite the clubs and societies formed on public courses in England and Wales and their course managements in the furtherance of the interests of the game. It is affiliated to the English Golf Union, and provides direct representation of public course interests to it.

Finally, there are some publicly available libraries and museums which have substantial collections of golf literature and artefacts, and as such are valuable sources of information. The national libraries within the United Kingdom all have substantial collections of golf books by virtue of the legal deposit law which requires that one copy of each publication should be provided by the publisher. These collections are of value as a place of last resort, and for the non-specialist user are not particularly easy to use. In general, specific titles are needed for requests to be serviced, and materials have to be used on the premises. The collections of the British Library in London and of the National Library of Scotland in Edinburgh both fall into this category. The specialist collection of the Greenwich Public Libraries in south east London is worthy of note. This library, through its participation in a London-wide special collections programme, is responsible for the collection of all books classified within the sports and recreation classes 790-799 of the Dewey Decimal Classification, and consequently holds a magnificent collection of over 500 volumes on golf. Many of these date back to the 1890s, and there is a very representative collection of the more important works published since that time. These books are held at the Plumstead Library in Greenwich, and are available for loan through any public library in the United Kingdom *via* the national inter-library loan systems. The London Library, a private subscription library in St. James's, Central London, also has a good collection of early golf books, many of which were donated by Lord Riddell. Much of the collection is earlier material and, although some items listed in the library's catalogue are missing, most are available for loan to members and to reading room subscribers on the library premises.

The Gullane Golf Museum, situated in Gullane village near to the famous Muirfield links some 20 miles from Edinburgh, is a small, but fascinating, collection of golfing artefacts. The museum traces the early history of the games from *circa* 1300, and covers implements, balls, the personalities, the costumes and other golfiana, including medals, buttons, paintings and pottery. The museum was established in 1980 and is open to the public daily throughout the summer months and at weekends in the winter. Another Scottish golf museum is the Spalding Golf Museum at Dundee. A catalogue of its exhibits and illustrations was published by the Dundee Corporation in 1968 under the title *Three centuries of golf.*

SELECT LIST OF ORGANISATIONS (all located in Britain except where otherwise indicated)

AMERICAN SOCIETY OF GOLF COURSE ARCHITECTS
221 North LaSalle Street, Chicago, Il 60601, USA Telephone (312) 372-7090

ASSOCIATION OF GOLF CLUB SECRETARIES
68 Chiltley Way, Liphook, Hampshire GU30 7HE Telephone (0428) 722009

BRITISH ASSOCIATION OF GOLF COURSE ARCHITECTS
c/o 18 Tierney Court, The Causeway, Marlow, Buckinghamshire Telephone (06284) 2234

BRITISH GOLF GREENKEEPERS' ASSOCIATION
7 Tenterden Close, Knaresborough, North Yorkshire HG5 9BJ Telephone (042376) 3851

CLUB MANAGERS ASSOCIATION OF AMERICA
7615 Winterberry Place, Washington DC 20034, USA Telephone (301) 229 3600

COUNCIL OF NATIONAL GOLF UNIONS
c/o Formby Golf Club, Formby, Liverpool L37 1LQ Telephone (07048) 72164

DEPARTMENTS OF THE ENVIRONMENT AND TRANSPORT, Library
2 Marsham Street, London SW1P 3EB Telephone (01) 212 4847

EDINBURGH CITY LIBRARIES
Central Library, George IV Bridge, Edinburgh EH1 1EG Scotland Telephone (031) 225 5584

ENGLISH GOLF UNION
12A Denmark Street, Wokingham, Berkshire RG11 2BE Telephone (0734) 781952

ENGLISH LADIES' GOLF ASSOCIATION
52 Boroughgate, Otley, West Yorkshire LS21 1QW Telephone (0943) 464010

EUROPEAN GOLF ASSOCIATION
69 avenue Victor-Hugo, 75783 Paris Cedex 16, France Telephone (331) 500 82 61

GOLF CLUB STEWARDS' ASSOCIATION
83 Wenwell Close, Aston Clinton, Aylesbury, Buckinghamshire Telephone (0296) 630224

GOLF COURSE BUILDERS' OF AMERICA INC
725 15th Street, NW, Washington, DC, 20005, USA Telephone (202) 638 0555

GOLF COURSE SUPERINTENDENTS' ASSOCIATION OF AMERICA
1617 St. Andrews Drive, Lawrence, Kansas 66044, USA Telephone (913) 841 2240

GOLF DEVELOPMENT COUNCIL
3 The Quadrant, Richmond, Surrey TW9 1BY Telephone (01) 940 0038

GOLF FOUNDATION LTD.
Allington House, 136-142 Victoria Street, London SW1E 5LD Telephone (01) 834 4688

GOLFING UNION OF IRELAND
Glencar House, 81 Eglinton Road, Donnybrook, Dublin 4, Eire Telephone (01) 694111

GREATER LONDON COUNCIL RESEARCH LIBRARY
Room 514, The County Hall, London SE1 7PB Telephone (01) 633 6068

GREENWICH LIBRARIES
Plumstead Library, Plumstead High Street, London SE18 Telephone (01) 854 1728

GULLANE GOLF MUSEUM
West Links Road, Gullane, East Lothian, Scotland Telephone (2277) 277

INSTITUTE OF PARK AND RECREATION ADMINISTRATION
Lower Basildon, Reading RG8 9NE Telephone (04914) 3558

INSTITUTE OF RECREATION MANAGEMENT
200 Sharncliffe Road, Folkestone, Kent CT20 2PH Telephone (0303) 52454

INTERNATIONAL ASSOCIATION OF GOLF ADMINISTRATORS
Box 51, Golf, Il 60029, USA

INTERNATIONAL GOLF ASSOCIATION
Time and Life Building, Room 4018, 101 West 50th Street, New York, NY 10020, USA Telephone (212) 551 2220

INTERNATIONAL GREENKEEPERS' ASSOCIATION
Via Golf, CH 6987, Caslano, Switzerland

LADIES' GOLF UNION
12 The Links, St. Andrews, Fife KY16 9JB, Scotland Telephone (0334) 75811

LADIES' PROFESSIONAL GOLF ASSOCATION
919 Third Avenue, 44th Floor, New York, NY 10033, USA Telephone (212)
751 8181

LEISURE STUDIES ASSOCIATION
Department of Extension Studies, Polytechnic of North London, Prince of
Wales Road, London NW5 3LB Telephone (01) 607 2789

LONDON LIBRARY
14 St. James's Square, London SW1 4LG Telephone (01) 930 7705

MEW RESEARCH
7 Layer Gardens, London W3 9PR Telephone (01) 992 6294

NATIONAL ASSOCIATION OF PUBLIC GOLF COURSES
161A Rye Lane, Peckham, London SE15 4TR Telephone (01) 639 8647

NATIONAL CLUB ASSOCIATION
1625 Eye Street, NW, Washington DC 20006, USA Telephone (202) 466 8424

NATIONAL GOLF CLUBS' ADVISORY ASSOCIATION
34 Sheen Road, Richmond, Surrey TW9 1AW Telephone (01) 940 7391

NATIONAL GOLF FOUNDATION INC.
200 Castlewood Drive, North Palm Beach, Fl 33408, USA Telephone (305)
844 2500

NATIONAL RECREATION AND PARKS ASSOCIATION
1200 Pennsylvania Avenue, NW, Washington DC 20006, USA Telephone
(202) 525 0606

PGA TOUR
100 Nina Court, Ponte Vedra Beach, Fl 32082, USA Telephone (904) 285
3700

PROFESSIONAL GOLFERS' ASSOCIATION
Apollo House, The Belfry, Sutton Coldfield B76 9PT Telephone (0675) 70333

PROFESSIONAL GOLFERS' ASSOCIATION. Tournament Players Division
c/o Wentworth Golf Club, Virginia Water, Surrey

PROFESSIONAL GOLFERS' ASSOCIATION OF AMERICA
804 Federal Highway, Lake Park, Fl 33403, USA Telephone (305) 844
5000

ROYAL AND ANCIENT GOLF CLUB OF ST. ANDREWS
St. Andrews, Fife KY16 9JD, Scotland Telephone (0334) 72112/3

SCOTTISH AND INTERNATIONAL GREENKEEPERS' ASSOCIATION
137 Saughtonhall Drive, Edinburgh EH12 5TS, Scotland Telephone (031) 337 3689

SCOTTISH GOLF UNION
Bank of Scotland Building, 54 Shandwick Place, Edinburgh EH2 4 RT, Scotland Telephone (031) 226 6711

SCOTTISH LADIES' GOLFING ASSOCIATION
1 Trinity Place, St. Andrews, Fife KY16 8SH, Scotland Telephone (0334) 76849

SCOTTISH SPORTS COUNCIL
1 St. Colme Street, Edinburgh EH3 6AA, Scotland Telephone (031) 225 8411

SPALDING GOLF MUSEUM
Camperdown Park, Dundee DD2 4JF, Scotland Telephone (0382) 645443

SPORTS COUNCIL
70 Brompton Road, London SW3 1EX Telephone (01) 589 3411

— East Midland Region
26 Musters Road, West Bridgford, Nottingham NG2 7PL Telephone (0602) 861325/6

— Eastern Region
26 Bromham Road, Bedford MK40 2QP Telephone (0234) 44281

— Greater London and South East Region
160 Great Portland Street, London W1N 5TB Telephone (01) 580 9092

— Northern Region
County Court Building, Hallgarth Street, Durham City DH1 3PB Telephone (0385) 64278

— North West Region
Byrom House, Quay Street, Manchester M3 5FJ Telephone (061) 834 0338
— South Western Region
Ashlands House, Crewkerne, Somerset TA18 7LQ Telephone (0460) 73491

— Southern Region
Watlington House, Watlington Street, Reading RG1 4RJ Telephone (0734) 52342

— West Midlands Region
Metropolitan House, 1 Hagley Road, Five Ways, Birmingham B16 8TT Telephone (021) 454 3808

— Yorkshire and Humberside Region
Coronet House, Queen Street, Leeds LS1 4PW Telephone (0532) 36443/4

SPORTS COUNCIL FOR NORTHERN IRELAND
49 Malone Road, Belfast BT9 6RZ, Northern Ireland Telephone (0232) 663154/662287

SPORTS COUNCIL FOR WALES
Sophia Gardens, Cardiff CF1 9SW, Wales Telephone (0222) 397571

SPORTS DOCUMENTATION CENTRE. University of Birmingham Library
PO Box 363, Edgbaston, Birmingham B15 2TT Telephone (021) 472 7410

SPORTS TURF RESEARCH INSTITUTE
Bingley, West Yorkshire BD16 1AU Telephone (09766) 5131

UNITED STATES GOLF ASSOCIATION
Golf House, Liberty Corner Road, Far Hills, NJ 07931, USA Telephone
(201) 234 2300

WELSH GOLFING UNION
2 Isfryn, Burry Port, Dyfed SA16 OBY, Wales Telephone (05546) 2595

WOMEN'S PROFESSIONAL GOLF ASSOCIATION
15 Cavendish Avenue, London NW8 Telephone (01) 286 8819

BIBLIOGRAPHY

Note: Annual reports, membership lists, constitutions and rule-books are produced by many associations and other bodies, though some are not available outside the membership. These are not listed.

AMERICAN INSTITUTE OF REAL ESTATE APPRAISERS
Golf courses: a guide to analysis and valuation.
Washington DC, Club Managers' Association of America, 1980.

AMERICAN SOCIETY OF GOLF COURSE ARCHITECTS
Master planning — the vital first steps in golf course construction.
Chicago, The Society, n.d. 12pp.

— Planning the municipal golf course.
Chicago, The Society, n.d. 9pp.

— Planning the real estate development golf course.
Chicago, The Society, n.d. 6pp.

— Selecting your golf course architect.
Chicago, The Society, n.d. 6pp.

BRITISH ASSOCIATION OF GOLF COURSE ARCHITECTS
Information bulletin.
Marlow, Bucks., The Association. First issue 1980 includes membership list and 30 text pages.

CLUB MANAGERS' ASSOCIATION OF AMERICA
Professional development for club managers.
Washington DC, The Association, n.d. 32pp. Catalogue of
services and publications available from the association.

DEPARTMENTS OF THE ENVIRONMENT AND TRANSPORT
Library bulletin.
London, The Departments, fortnightly. Abstract bulletin of
articles and publications relevant to environmental matters
and including material on sports and recreation.

GOLF COURSE BUILDERS OF AMERICA INC.   Yearbook
and directory.
Annual.

GOLF COURSE SUPERINTENDENTS' ASSOCIATION OF
AMERICA   Profile of golf course superintendents.
Lawrence, Kansas, The Association, 1979. 12pp.

GOLF DEVELOPMENT COUNCIL   Analyses of current costs.
Richmond, Surrey, The Council.

— Golf clubhouses: a planning guide.
Richmond, Surrey, The Council.

GREATER LONDON COUNCIL   Urban abstracts.
London, The Council. Monthly. Abstract bulletin containing
material selected from periodicals, and listing local government and other publications. Includes a small amount of
relevant material on sports and recreation, especially the
planning and provision aspects. The ACOMPLIS
(Computerised London Information Service) database is
also produced by the Research Library of the Greater
London Council, and includes similar material.

INSTITUTE OF RECREATION MANAGEMENT   Recreation
management directory.
Third edition London, Spon, 1981.

NATIONAL RECREATION AND PARKS ASSOCIATION
Bibliography of theses and dissertations in recreation, parks,
camping and outdoor education.
Washington DC, The Association, 1970.

— Par-3 golf.
Washington DC, The Association, n.d. (Management aids
series)

SCOTTISH LADIES' GOLFING ASSOCIATION   History of
the Scottish Ladies' Golfing Association, 1903-1928, compiled
by Noel Dunlop-Hill.
London, Mortons, 1929. 62pp.

SCOTTISH SPORTS COUNCIL   The teaching of golf in
schools: conference arranged by the Scottish Sports Council in
conjunction with the Golf Development Council at Stirling,
6 May 1976.
Edinburgh, The Council, 1976. 11pp.

SPALDING GOLF MUSEUM   Three centuries of golf: the
story of golf.
Dundee, Dundee Corporation, 1968. 12pp. Catalogue of
exhibits and illustrations from the Spalding Golf Museum,
Dundee.

SPORTS COUNCIL, Eastern Region   Provision for sport in the
Eastern region: existing and proposed purpose-built sports
facilities in counties and districts.
Bedford, The Council, 1978. 9pp.

—, East Midland Region *and* GOLF DEVELOPMENT COUNCIL
Provision, finance and management of public golf courses:
conference arranged by the Sports Council East Midlands
Region and the Golf Development Council at Holme Pierrepoint,
Nottingham, 5 April 1973. Nottingham, The Council, 1973.
69pp.

— Greater London and South East Region   Provision, finance and management of golf facilities for public use: conference arranged by the Greater London and the South East Sports Council, London, 19 November 1973.
London, The Council, 1973. 41pp.

— North West Region   Directory of facilities 1978.
Manchester, The Council, 1978. (Recreation strategy technical report no. 2)

— West Midlands Region   Report to West Midlands Council for Sport and Recreation Technical (Planning) Panel Steering Committee by Golf Course Working Party.
Birmingham, The Council, 197?. 18pp.

SPORTS COUNCIL FOR WALES.   Golf courses in Wales.
Cardiff, The Council, 1979?

SPORTS DOCUMENTATION CENTRE. University of Birmingham Library   Sports documentation monthly bulletin.
Monthly. 1970-.

UNITED STATES GOLF ASSOCIATION   A brief introduction to the museum and library of the United States Golf Association
Far Hills, NJ, The Association, 1974. 16pp.

WELSH GOLFING UNION   Seventy fifth anniversary souvenir report.
[no location], The Union, 1970. 69pp.

COLLECTING
GOLFIANA

As this book, and Joseph Murdoch's *Library of golf* (1968), indicates there are many books and other documentary sources of information on the game of golf. There are also many other items — *objets d'art* and ephemera — which make a significant contribution to the overall understanding of the game and of the social *milieu* in which it has been played over time. Although there are millions of players relatively few of them seem to be aware of the beauty and interest of so many other items associated with the game, though there is considerable evidence of a substantial growth in the serious collecting of golfiana.

This brief essay is not an attempt to classify chronologically all golfing curios. It is designed rather to provide an introduction to the enjoyments to be obtained from collecting golf-related items.

Collecting of golf clubs and balls is one of the most popular fields, and many collectors are primarily interested in this area. The earliest club shafts were made of wood — possibly hazel or thorncuts. Hickory, which was used until the development of steel shafts around 1930, seems to have first arrived from America in the 1850s, and Robert Forgan, a clubmaker from St. Andrews, was the first to use this material. Most early drivers, putters, niblicks, brassies and mashies were made in wood, but there are records of some being made in iron. The Troon and Royal Blackheath Golf Clubs have examples in their collections. The best clubs were all patented and have numbers which enable identification of the makers. Famous clubmakers included William Ballantyne of Musselburgh (1793-1845), G. Forrester of Elie in Fife (1847-1930), Robert Forgan of St. Andrews (1824-1900), Tom Morris of Prestwick and St. Andrews (1821-1906), Willie Park senior of Musselburgh (1834-1903) and his son Mungo. Special

1 Art Deco lady golfer and caddie. Maker unknown, 1920s.

clubs for ladies were made and are slightly lighter and shorter and sometimes marked with a letter *L* on the face of the club. Children's clubs were also made, particularly in America, and are often scarce items. Earlier clubs in good condition are often extremely valuable, and prices can run into hundreds of pounds. Early golf balls, both of the "feathery" and gutta percha type, are also much sought after by collectors. Each feather ball contained a top hat full of boiled feathers in a leather stitched case. They were in use up to about 1850. After that time the "guttie" was used, as it was cheaper to produce, until the invention of the modern style of ball around the beginning of the twentieth century.

2 *Royal Doulton urn (eleven inches high and eleven inches across at the widest point).*

Delft tiles (*circa* 1650) were the first ceramic pieces depicting golfing scenes, and these are extremely rare. Much more recent ceramics of interest include the Copeland Spode teapot and loving cup, dated around 1910, which is in royal blue with a white raised design of five golfers in action (3). Royal Doulton, around the beginning of the twentieth century, were probably the most prolific

3 Copeland Spode teapot in royal blue and white c 1910.

of all the ceramic designers, with the famous Crombie illustrations (2). A dinner service shows coloured transfers of players in Jacobean dress, and the set includes dinner plates, tea plates, cups and saucers, a punchbowl, vases from 3 to 12 inches in height, and dishes in all shapes. A teapot, milk jug and loving cup, dated 1916, all have a silver rim (4). All have "sayings" added. These words of wisdom include "Promise little and do much", "He that always complains is never pitied", "He hath a good judgement who relieth not wholly on his own", "All fools are not knaves but all knaves are fools" and "Give losers leave to speak and winners to laugh". Royal Doulton also made a stoneware jug in dark brown with three golf scenes in white. Another teaset has a green border with a golfer talking to his caddie and the legend "Holing out". The transfer suggests this is Wedgwood with a date around 1920. Doulton were also well known for commissioning famous illustrators, such as Cecil Gibson, to design china. His most famous piece shows two players resting with a caddie looking on, and is entitled "Is a caddie really necessary" (5). Royal Worcester transposed the famous Blackheath Golfers (1916) to a six inch high mug. This golfing picture has probably been reproduced more times than any other, as is indicated later in this appendix.

4 *Royal Doulton "Crombie" series with silver rim dated 1916*

W.H. Goss created a match holder in circular form with a golf emblem which is now a rare item. Carltonware made a cream coloured holder with a golfer in plus fours and a caddie in the background. A rare match striker depicts the famous Tom Morris in a brown jacket and peak cap with his caddie carrying his putter over his shoulder. The background shows mountains which are probably Scotland. Carltonware also commissioned John Hassall to design a caddie in black plus fours and a red jacket, and having a head, in the shape of a golf ball, loose on a piece of string so that it can be placed at any angle. The caddie is holding a putter at the ready (6). Tobacco jars and bowls were also made by Doulton as well as by other manufacturers. Some of these are very attractive and colourful pieces: one example slowly turned depicts the whole golf course from tee to green.

5 *Cecil Gibson drawings on a Royal Doulton vase (left) and a postcard (right).*

215

Crested china, other than that designed by Goss, includes golf balls with varied crests, caddies measuring only two and a half inches, a golf bag with clubs, and a caddie standing on a golf ball. Arcadian china made a miniature milk jug featuring the Alnmouth Golf Club crest. In the centre of this piece is a golfer, one and a half inches high, addressing the ball. Grimswade produced a tea service with "The Brownies" playing golf. The teapot is a squat shape in delicate colours showing seven golfers. It has an inscription on the base explaining that "Brownies are imaginary little sprites who delight in harmless pranks and helpful deeds. They work and sport while many households sleep and are never seen by mortal eyes". Macintyre of Burslem produced a dish that probably belonged to a golf club where the members were keen bridge players. It is in the shape of the ace of clubs. In the centre is a golfer in sepia at the top of his swing. This piece is dated 1910.

6 *Carltonware caddie designed by John Hassall.*

7 *Royal Doulton tobacco jar.*

Cruet sets have been produced in all materials, especially silver, brass and china, and usually in the shape of golf balls. One china set, known to the writer, has a small caddie carrying his clubs across his back with the usual three golf balls around him. The set is housed on a green leaf-shaped dish. Golf is also depicted on many ashtrays. Other smoking-related items include a pipe moulded in the form of long-headed wooden clubs with gutty balls on the top. Table lighters are often golf balls with a club lying across the front, while cigarette boxes are frequently found in the form of a casket with different scenes of courses and play. Jewellery for both men and women often has golfing motifs. Some pieces show golf bags and clubs in gold and silver, or use crossed clubs as a pendant or brooch. A single club, with a pearl or diamond, is sometimes found in a tie pin. Competition medals, cufflinks and buttons are decorative, and are often specific to particular golf clubs. Many clubs have their own ties, and also badges for wearing on blazers. There are also the "hole in one" ties for those clever enough (or lucky enough!) to qualify for membership of the appropriate society. Toastracks are usually made of silver (or electroplated nickel silver (EPNS)) in the shape of six crossed clubs standing on four golf balls. They usually have an extra club and ball in the centre which enables the user to pick up the rack when full of toast (8). Inkwells and inkstands sometimes have a centrepiece of a golfer about to strike a ball.

Car mascots depict golfers with clubs, and are usually from two to eight inches tall. Desmo made a flying golf ball (c.1930), and the Lucifer Golfing Society have a flat medal trophy mascot. The Dunlop Company produced a plaster of paris golfer some 15 inches high, in which the head is a golfball. For party-givers, there is a chocolate mould showing a rabbit carrying a golf bag containing clubs. Jelly moulds with golfing shapes have also been made. There are also card games such as Kargo, and ordinary packs of playing cards featuring famous golfers.

The firm of Huntley and Palmer, whose chief product is biscuits, produced a tin with golfing scenes on it, but the most attractive of this genre is "The golf bag" by Macfarlane Lang, which was issued in 1913 and measured ten and a half inches. The golfer's stance and follow-through is splendidly portrayed; he cuts a dashing figure embossed against a leather golf bag complete with ball and tee pouch, and attired in Harris tweeds and green plus fours. The reverse side of the tin shows his lady companion just one shot behind!

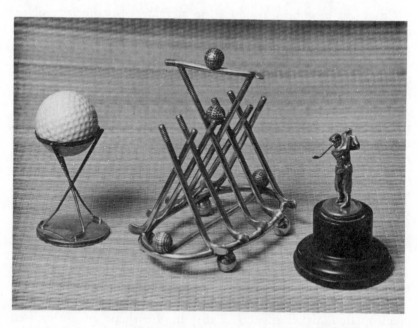

8 Left to right: silver ball holder; EPNS toastrack; silver statuette.

Silver spoons vary in design from the simple, straightforward club shaft to the elegant and elaborate engraved enamel heads (9). Sets of six spoons are now rarely found. A typical example of a set (made in 1939) has lady golfers carved at the top of the shanks. Another pair of spoons has an older golfer carved at the top, with a plaited shaft, while the bowl of the spoon, when reversed, is pitted as in a golf ball. Many spoons have only the initials of the golf club they originated from, and are often difficult to identify. Trophies and salvers, which have been presented as prizes for club events, are frequently made of silver, as are cups, serviette rings and egg cups. Manicure sets have been produced with six different implements housed in a leather golf bag, and cocktail sticks are usually modelled on the different shapes of golf clubs in a bag. Silver vesta boxes (9) and match strikers are often elaborately chased and some have beautifully painted enamel fronts. Menu holders can be small clubs from one to four inches in height. Photograph frames are made in wood or silver: some are very small, for example, one an inch and a half square is known to the writer, "chased" with clubs. A replica of this is also available in brass. Tape measures are made in the shape of a ball, with a club for rewinding purposes. Swiss-made fob watches in the form of "gutty balls" have been collected, and are made in EPNS.

9 *Silver matchstriker and six silver spoons.*

There are statues of many well-known golfers in both bronze and silver (8). They vary in size from 5 to 25 inches in height, and were produced around the beginning of the twentieth century. Marble bookends, mounted with bronze figures of golfers and caddies, were current around the year 1920. The smallest known figure was made by the toy manufacturers, Britains, in their railway set. This set includes two golfers, each about half an inch high, one carrying his bag of clubs in his hand and the other with his bag over his shoulder. The figures are hollow and made of lead. There is also a larger version of both of these (around one and a half inches high) with one golfer carrying a single club. The rarest figure Britains made is one about five inches high. Louis Marx, an American firm, also made golfing toys (10). One of these is a golfer standing on the green putting the ball into nine different holes. The ingenious clockwork mechanism allows the ball to return to the player each time it is played. Another shows a five inch high caddie in pressed tin. Table-top miniature games and board games can also be found with golfing themes. Walking sticks and parasols have been moulded into all the different iron and wooden clubs, with some very ornately carved with silver. Golfing glassware is available etched with handpainted scenes. Brandy goblets have been produced with similar scenes of golfers and courses. One example recently examined by the writer was a 12 inch high balloon glass. It was probably a club trophy of some kind, though no event details were engraved on it. Steins and beer mugs have also been collected, often from as far back as 1890.

Golfing ephemera form a vast and delightful area of collecting, particularly in the realm of paper materials. It is such a wide-ranging field that it is often difficult to know how to set any limits from the collecting point of view. There are, however, so many interesting oddities that are easily lost or destroyed but which do deserve preservation, if only because of the sidelights they provide, both on the social history of the period from which they originate as well as on the development of the game. Post-cards are part of a larger, and more generalised collecting field, but there are many specifically of interest to golfers. Famous artists have produced postcards depicting golfing activities, and these include G.E. Studdy, Phil May, Lawson Woods, Cecil Aldin, Tom Browne, Mabel Lucie Attwell, Chloe Preston and Harry Rountree. Some of the most attractive early postcards show the early stars such as Tom Morris, and there is one portraying James Braid when he became Open Champion in 1906. There are also many showing lady golfers in the period from 1900 to 1970 (5). These make a valuable contribution to the rather neglected area of the history of golfing apparel. Some Christmas cards, often unsigned, have golf as their theme. A personal favourite is a three-dimensional card with verse. Cigarette cards are also a major collecting field in their own right, and some have particular interest to the collector of golfiana. The tobacco company Churchmans issued a set of 12 famous golfers, while Millhof's set with the same title included 27 cards. Cope's issued a set showing golf strokes, as did Morris's. One of the rarest sets is by Cope Brothers and is a large-size set of 50 cards, simply entitled "Cope's golfers".

Golf score cards are also collected. They can provide an interesting historical record, especially when examples of completed and signed cards from important tournaments can be found. Much more inexpensive is the collection of unused, or used, scorecards from golf courses played by the collector.

Music sheet covers have also featured golf, and one of the most famous is Kerr's Song Book of 1893. Other examples are entitled "Fore" and the "Gleneagles foxtrot". In photographs it is often difficult to identify the golfers shown. Some particularly interesting sets are those produced by the independent British railway companies of the 1920s, which show some of the seaside courses

10 *Two golf toys (left) by an unknown maker, (right) by Louis Marx.*

in their territories. These were displayed in the carriages of the time. The interest of the railway companies in promoting golfing tourism at about this time has already been noted in an earlier chapter of this sourcebook. Similarly, books of golfing cartoons have been mentioned, though some of the best are to be found in the general magazines and have, in many cases, not been collected for separate publication. "Spy" cartoons in *Vanity Fair* are well known, with golfers featured among the caricatures. Mure Fergusson is in the issue for 18 June 1903, John Ball, junior appears in the issue of 5 March, 1893, and the Hoylake Golf Course is shown in the issue for 16 July 1903.

Golf championship programmes, especially those autographed by leading players, are sought after, as are posters advertising the events. Original water colours and oil paintings, many featuring clubhouses, are also scarce items. The Aikman etchings of Scottish golf links are particularly interesting and exceptionally rare. One of the most famous paintings (as mentioned earlier) is the Blackheath Golfers, showing the golfer and his caddie. It was painted by L.F. Abbott around 1790 and is often reproduced. The *Illustrated London News*, and similar magazines, have also published many golf illustrations, and those of the Victorian era and of the early years of the twentieth century are particularly interesting. In more recent times, national postage stamps have featured golfing themes and personalities; these include Jersey's showing Harry Vardon and South Africa's depicting Gary Player. There have been first day covers on the British Open championship and in the United States an issue showing Bobby Jones and sport appeared. There have been films in which golf is featured, and of particular interest to the collector of golfing ephemera are the "front-of-house" stills and posters for these. Two fairly recent examples are "Caddy" featuring Jerry Lewis, and "Caddyshack". The *Chicago Tribune* (June 1926) carried an excellent front page cover of Bobby Jones, as well as several of the P.G. Wodehouse golf stories illustrated in colour. The *Girls Own annual* (1931) has a rare dustwrapper showing a lady golfer on the cover and spine. The Guinness Company have featured golf in their very effective advertising. In their 1935 scrapbook they included four H.M. Bateman cartoons related to the subject. Another excellent example from this company is a black and white poster showing the White Rabbit from Lewis Carroll's *Alice in wonderland* holding a broken wooden club and saying "Guinness is good for your golf".

This brief overview is obviously selective, and the examples mentioned are only a small part of the *memorabilia* that is extant. There is considerable scope for the collector of golfiana; it is an enjoyable, stimulating and sometimes lucrative pastime.

ABBREVIATIONS

Al	Alabama	Pa	Pennsylvania
Ariz	Arizona	*pp.*	pages
Berks	Berkshire	*pseud.*	pseudonym
Bucks	Buckinghamshire	RI	Rhode Island
Ca	California	SA	South Africa
Co	Company	Tx	Texas
comp.	compiler	UK	United Kingdom
Corp	Corporation	Va	Virginia
Ct	Connecticut	Vt	Vermont
DC	District of Columbia	Wash	Washington (state)
ed.	editor	Wis	Wisconsin
Fl	Florida	Yorks	Yorkshire
Herts	Hertfordshire		
Il	Illinois		
Ind	Indiana		
Kan	Kansas		
Ma	Massachusetts		
Mi	Michigan		
Minn	Minnesota		
NC	North Carolina		
nd	no date		
NJ	New Jersey		
NSW	New South Wales		
NY	New York (state)		
NZ	New Zealand		
Oh	Ohio		
Or	Oregon		
P	Press		
p	periodical		

TITLE INDEX

225

228

229

237

238

NAME AND
SUBJECT INDEX

248

249

251